Threat Prevention Approach for Maintaining Protected Payload Exchange in a Sensing Architecture

Dominus

Threat Prevention Approach for Maintaining Protected Payload Exchange in a Sensing Architecture

First Edition June 2025

Written by Dominus

TABLE OF CONTENTS

CHAPTER NO.	TITLE	PAGE NO.

1	INTRODUCTION	1
	1.1 INTRODUCTION	1
	1.2 INTRUSION DETECTION SYSTEMS 1.3	5
	INTRUSION DETECTION SYSTEM	
	TYPES	8
	1.3.1 Network Based IDS	8
	1.3.2 Host Based IDS	10
	1.3.3 Application Protocol Based IDS	11
	1.3.4 Signature Based IDS	11
	1.3.5 Anomaly Based IDS	11
	1.3.6 Wireless	12
	1.3.7 Network Behavior Analysis (NBA)	12
	1.4 INTRUSION DETECTION SYSTEM	
	REQUIREMENTS	12
	1.4.1 Information Required for Detection	12
	1.4.2 Derived IDS Requirements	18
	1.5 INTRUSION ATTACKS	18
	1.5.1 Types of Intrusion Attacks	19

CHAPTER NO.	TITLE	PAGE NO.
	1.6 TYPES OF INTRUSION DETECTION TECHNIQUES	22
	1.6.1 Anomaly Based Intrusion Detection Technique	22
	1.6.2 Signature Based Intrusion Detection	24
	1.6.3 Specification Based Intrusion Detection	25
	1.7 PROBLEM DEFINITION	26
	1.8 OBJECTIVE	26
	1.9 RESEARCH CONTRIBUTION	27
	1.10 ORGANIZATION OF THE THESIS	27
	1.11 SUMMARY	28
2	LITERATURE REVIEW	29
	2.1 INTRODUCTION	29
	2.2 REVIEW ON SECURITY ISSUES IN WIRELESS SENSOR NETWORK	30
	2.3 REVIEW ON INTRUSION DETECTION SYSTEM	42
	2.4 REVIEW ON OPTIMIZATION ALGORITHM IN INTRUSION DETECTION	53
	2.5 SUMMARY	63
3	INTRUSION AWARE DATA TRANSMISSION FRAMEWORK IN WIRELESS SENSOR NETWORK	64
	3.1 INTRODUCTION	65
	3.2 SECURED DATA TRANSMISSION FRAMEWORK	66
	3.3 FEATURE EXTRACTIONS	68

CHAPTER NO.	TITLE	PAGE NO.
	3.4 FEATURE GROUPING USING FUZZY BASED MEAN SHIFT CLUSTERING	69
	3.5 DECISION MAKING USING GENETIC NEURO CLASSIFIER	73
	3.6 OPTIMAL ROUTE PATH SELECTION	77
	3.6.1 Fitness Evaluation	80
	3.7 RESULTS AND DISCUSSION	81
	3.8 SUMMARY	87
4	SECONDARY SERVER-BASED COMPUTATION OVERHEAD REDUCED FRAGMENTATION ATTACK DETECTION IN WIRELESS SENSOR NETWORK	88
	4.1 INTRODUCTION	88
	4.2 SECONDARY SERVER-BASED FRAGMENTATION ATTACK DETECTION	90
	4.3 SECONDARY SERVER SELECTION USING IMPROVED GENETIC ALGORITHM	92
	4.3.1 Improved Genetic Algorithm	93
	4.4 BIAS AND VARIANCE ESTIMATION	94
	4.5 TRUNCATED SVM FOR ATTACK LEARNING AND DETECTION	96
	4.6 OPTIMAL ROUTE PATH SELECTION USING MODIFIED MOSQUITO SWARM ALGORITHM	98
	4.7 SECURITY USING MODIFIED DOUBLE KEY ENCRYPTION	100
	4.7.1 First Level Encryption	103

CHAPTER NO.	TITLE	PAGE NO.

4.7.2 Second Level Encryption 103

4.8 RESULTS AND DISCUSSION 104

4.9 SUMMARY 109

5 COMPUTATION OVERHEAD REDUCED, AND PRIVACY CONCERNED SECURED ROUTING IN WIRELESS SENSOR NETWORK 110

5.1 INTRODUCTION 110

5.2 COMPUTATION OVERHEAD REDUCED PRIVACY CONCERNED DATA TRANSMISSION 110

5.3 SECONDARY SERVER SELECTION USING MODIFIED SQUIRREL SEARCH ALGORITHM 112

5.4 ANONYMOUS AUTHENTICATION 118

5.4.1 Random Value Generation Phase 119

5.4.2 Secret Key Generation and Sharing Phase 120

5.4.3 Authentication Phase 122

5.5 OPTIMAL ROUTE PATH SELECTION USING ANARCHY SOCIETY OPTIMIZATION ALGORITHM 123

5.5.1 Trust Level Estimation 123

5.5.2 Route Path Construction Using Anarchy Society Optimization 125

5.6 DATA ENCRYPTION USING TRIPLE LEVEL ENCRYPTION 127

5.7 RESULTS AND DISCUSSION 129

5.8 SUMMARY 134

CHAPTER NO.	TITLE	PAGE NO.
6	CONCLUSION AND FUTURE WORK	135
	6.1 CONCLUSION	135
	6.2 FUTURE WORK	136
	REFERENCES	137

CHAPTER 1

INTRODUCTION

1.1 INTRODUCTION

Peer-to-peer networks and client server networks are the two categories into which networks may be divided according to network management (Chen et al. 2020) An administrator of the network or the system is responsible for maintaining network security. The safety policy is put into action by the administration, by availing the hardware and network software required to prevent unwanted accessing to a network and the assets accessible over the network. The Internet and other modern networking technologies have increased the world's connectivity. The varied networking infrastructures in this wide global world is stored with a significant quantity of information that is personal, commercial, military, and governmental in nature. The ease with which one may get intellectual property via the usage of the internet is one of the primary factors contributing to the growing significance of network security. A security system for a network will often use numerous levels of protection and will be comprised of various components. These components will typically combine hardware and appliances with networking monitoring and security software. Each component contributes, in concert with the others, to the overall strengthening of the computer network's defenses.

Data security refers to the feature of information security that enables the data belonging to a customer to be changed into data that cannot be understood during transmission (Jadaun et al. 2021). The once-robust methods of encryption may now be cracked with relative ease. Because of the ongoing development of hacking techniques, cryptographic protocols are required to undergo constant improvement. When exchanging encrypted text across a network, having a secure network is of great assistance and is recommended. A secure network will also prevent unauthorized communications from being added to the network by preventing someone from adding them. Therefore, there is a need for hard ciphers in addition to attack hard networks.

A group of networks make up the internet. From everywhere, one is able to gather and exchange data. Employing secured private networks or intranets is becoming more common among businesses due to concerns about security breaches on the Internet. Security features have been added to the Internet Protocol Suite's different levels by the Internet Engineering Task Force (IETF). Internet security has been standardized through the internet protocol's security architecture, or IP Security. Securing networks have multiple facets, one of which is computer security at each link in the communication chain. While doing so, data transmission routes shouldn't be vulnerable to attack. An aspiring attacker can decide to target the communications channel, acquire the information, decode it, and then reintroduce a fake statement. Network security is the same as important as safeguarding PCs from danger and encrypting communications (Diro et al. 2018). Five major components should be taken into account while creating a secure network: gaining network access, discretion, Validation, Reliability and Refusal of rebuke.

There are four key components to computer security. These points have previously been covered, although in a somewhat different manner, but are restated for prominence and clarification. These security traits include confidence, consistency, security, and reliability.

Table 1.1 Security Traits

Characteristics of	Attacking techniques used	Internet security technologies
Confidenriality	DOS, Eavesdropping and Hacking, IP spoofing and Phishing	Intrusion Detection Systems (IDSs), Firewalls, Cryptography, IP Security and SSSL
Reliability	Virus/Worm/Trojan attacks, DOS, Eavesdropping, IP spoofing	IDSs, Firewalls Anti-Malwares, IP Security and SSSL
Privacy	Email bombs, spam, hacks, DOS, Cookies	IDSs, Firewalls Anti-Malwares, IP Security and SSSL
Accessibility	Email bombs, spam, hacks, DOS, Cookies and infecting boot records	IDSs, Firewalls Anti-Malwares

Considering that it is challenging to continuously check the sensor nodes and network, security is seen to be the most difficult challenge in WSN (Singh & Saini 2021). But it must be protected to stop a hacker from assaulting the data flow. The most often used words in security are attack and attacker. Anyone who attempts to manipulate information or gains unauthorized access to network data is considered an attacker. A network attack occurs when an attacker uses its services. WSN is constructed using layers. These defenses aid in shielding the sensor from different assaults.

Security problems in wireless sensor networks were various, but some are common. These include the topology's tendency to change dynamically, the sensor nodes' reliance on wireless communication, the framework's lack of infrastructure, and the scarce physical resources such as energy, memory, and communication bandwidth that they can use. For safe data transfer and routing in WSN, several analysts presented numerous threats handling models and different security procedures.

In order to provide secure communication, sensor networks must satisfy a number of conditions. Authentication, availability, secrecy, and integrity are the general security criteria for WSNs. Source localization, self-organization, and data freshness are some additional criteria that are referred as secondary needs. These criteria safeguard the data delivered through the sensor network against assaults.

Data Confidentiality: Data goes across several intermediary nodes in sensor networks, increasing the likelihood of data leakage. Encrypted data is used to guarantee data secrecy, and only the receiver is able to decode the data to restore it to its original form.

Data Integrity: Data quality indicates that no changes or modifications should be made to the data that the receiver receives. It's possible that an outsider or an unfriendly atmosphere changed the initial data. When transmitting the information to the receiver, the intruding party has the ability to change it to suit its purposes. Data Verification is the process of verifying the sender of the communicating node verifying if the data received from an authentic node is crucial for the receiving node.

Data Availability: When one talks about data availability, it is implied that the services remain accessible at all times, even in the face of threats like denial of service assaults. Source Localization: Some apps use the sink node's location details to their benefit while transmitting data. It is crucial to make sure that the location data is kept confidential. Data that is not encrypted may be manipulated by the rogue node if it sends signals with a fake signal strength or replays signals.

Self-Organization: In a WSN, there is no permanent infrastructure, and as a result, The network's nodes are all independent and capable of adapt to various circumstances, as well as the capacity to self-organize and self-heal. When it comes to WSN security, this presents a significant difficulty.

Data Freshness: The communication is considered to be "fresh" according to the phrase "data" that is sent over the channel is brand new. It ensures that the previous messages will never be repeated by any node in the network. This problem may be overcome by including a time-related counter in order to determine whether the data has been recently updated.

1.2 INTRUSION DETECTION SYSTEMS

Information systems are protected by Intrusion Detection Systems (IDSs), which are utilized in combination with other preventive safety precautions, such as accessibility limitation and validation. There are several reasons to include IDS in the protection system. First, conventional applications and systems were created without considering security. In other instances, systems or apps that were created to function in a variety of situations are susceptible when used. ID supplements defenses to increase system security. It is useful to be aware of intrusions that have happened or are currently occurring in order to better comprehend security dangers and hazards and to be better prepared for assaults in the future, even if preventative security procedures effectively safeguard information systems.

Numerous IDS prototypes have been developed since Denning's groundbreaking work in 1981. A partial list of 59 of them is kept by Sobriety. IDS is an emerging computer security area due to issues in ensuring that information systems are of security flaws. Computer systems do, in fact, contain security vulnerabilities regardless of their intended use, manufacturer, or place of origin, according to the taxonomy of security problems. Aside from being monetarily expensive, ensuring that computer networks and systems are secure, is also technically challenging. IDSs gather information for security assessments (Sahasrabuddhe et al. 2017) for covering up breaches or weaknesses that may turn into breaches.

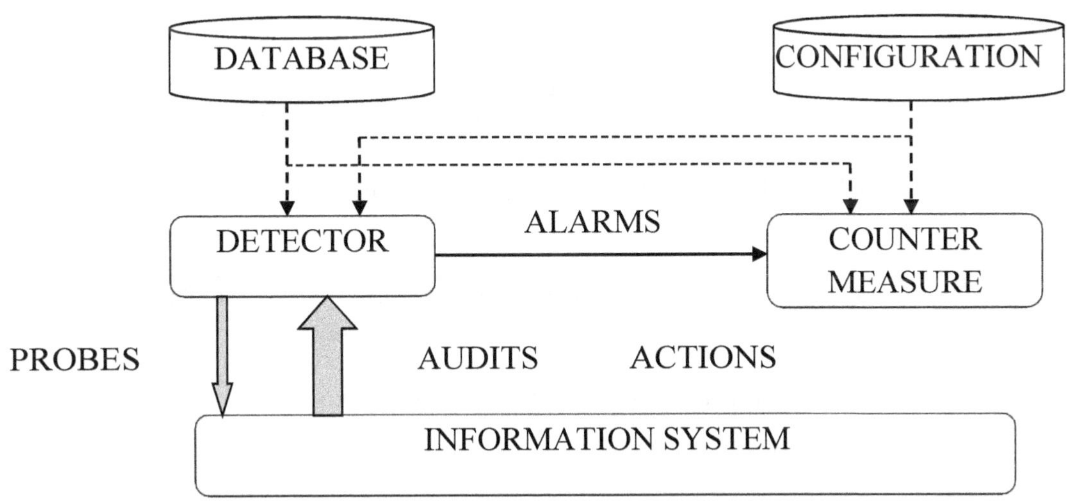

Figure 1.1 Simple Intrusion Detection Systems

IDSs are detectors that process inputs originating from systems for protections at macroscopic levels (Figure 1.1). These detector have the capability to run probes that audit apps which demanding version numbers. They make use of three categories of information including visional information on intrusion identifications (an assaults knowledge base), configuration information regarding the state the system is now in, and audit records outlining system-related occurrences. The detector's task is to obliterate extraneous information from an audit trail that displays a synthetic view of security-related activities that were naturally carried out while using the system or a synthetic picture of the system's actual security condition. It is decided to assess the likelihood that certain behaviors or states constitute signs of intrusions or vulnerabilities. In order to stop operations from being executed or to alter the system state to a secure one, a mitigation element makes correction measures.

IDS aid information systems in attack prevention and response. In order to do this, they gather information from multiple networks and systems, analyze them, and look for potential weaknesses in safety. Detection of intrusions offers:

- Observing and evaluating user and system activities
- Monitoring of system settings and flaws
- Integrity evaluation of important system and data files
- Examination of activity patterns using statistics to compare them to known attacks
- Observation of unusual behavior
- Operating system evaluation

There are 3 components in IDS (Meena & Choudhary 2017):

- Network Intrusion Detection system (NIDS)- examines all of the subnet's active traffic. Matches traffic on subnets to a database of known attacks in a promiscuous manner. An alert is delivered to the administrator when a threat is detected or aberrant activity is noticed.

- Network Node Intrusion Detection System (NNIDS) – examines network traffic that is sent to a certain host. The difference between NIDS and NNIDS is that just a single host is watched for traffic, not the whole subnet.

- Host Intrusion Detection System (HIDS)- comparing a present sample of the system files to an earlier one. In the event that critical system files were modified or deleted, the administrator is informed and should look into it.

1.3 INTRUSION DETECTION SYSTEM TYPES

There are many ways to categorize IDS types available (Anwar et al. 2017). Based on transactions, activities, traffic or systems monitored, Network-based (NIDS), host-based (HIDS), and application-based (APIDS) systems are the three subcategories of IDS. IDS differentiates between Signature-based (SIDS) and Anomaly-based systems based on various event analysis methodologies. Each IDS type hasits own unique advantages and disadvantages.

1.3.1 Network Based IDS

The Network Intrusion Detection System (NIDS) monitors is accountable for all incoming and outgoing network traffic (Subba et al. 2016). They connect to the network via various hubs and network taps.

- They examine entering network packets looking for abnormal patterns.

- They look for internal intruders by scanning outgoing communications. The monitoring of incoming and outgoing traffic and the presence of NIDS at network nodes slow down the network's overall performance.

NIDS has traffic processing restrictions despite its value:

- NIDS issues on switched network in the environment (Tran-Thanh et al. 2018). In contrast to hub-based networks, it delivers packets exclusively to the designated receiver directly by designing switch functionalities. Spreading ports (often used for debugging) or network taps are used to counteract this. All communication sent by the switch is received by the port. The figure 1.2 indicates the NIDS implementation.

- When installing IDS on high-speed networks, speed is a crucial consideration since weak IDS won't be able to collect all traffic when the limit is surpassed. Furthermore, an attacker may overwhelm a network with traffic while going undetected. Appliance solutions (specific hardware) have been developed by vendors to enhance its performance.

- Networks that are encrypted: Because SSH communication is encrypted, NIDS cannot warn the administrator when an attacker connects to a workstation using this method. HIDS determines behavior evolution on the machine.

NIDS Implementation

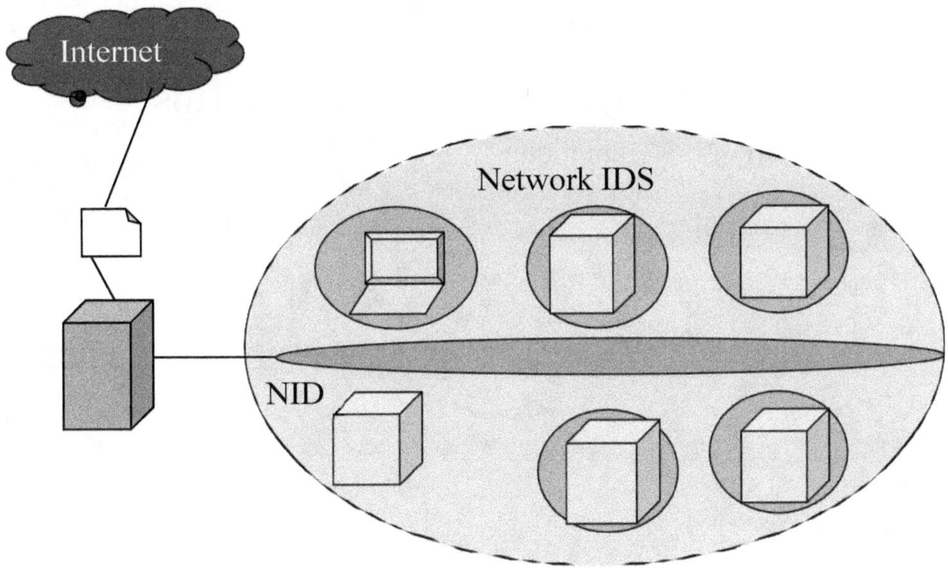

Figure 1.2 NIDS implementation

1.3.2 Host Based IDS

HIDS keeps track of in a specific network system, the incoming and outgoing traffic (Haider et al. 2016). It pays close attention to the status of the computer system and dynamic behavior in particular. The figure 1.3 represents the HIDS implementation.

- The administrator is notified when intrusion is detected

- NIDS is used with HIDS to identify activities that HIDS overlooked

HIDS Implementation

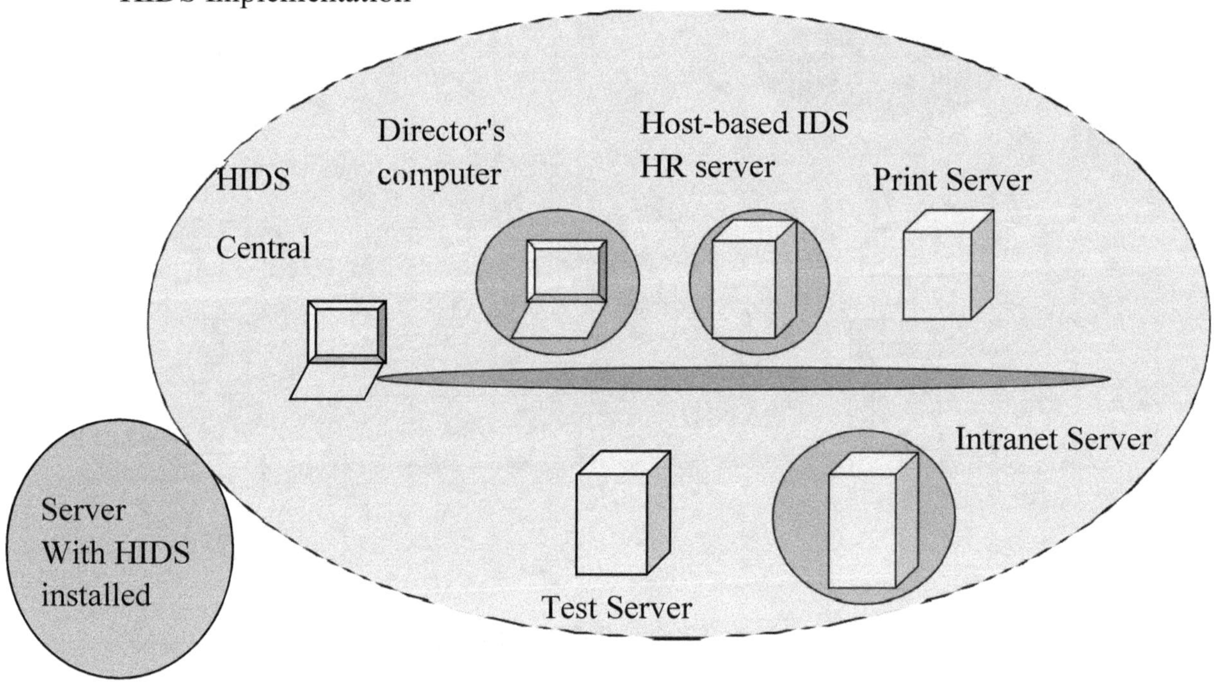

Figure 1.3 HIDS Implementation

1.3.3 Application Protocol Based IDS

APIDS keeps track of activities in certain computer system protocols. It seeks protocols and enforces correct system use.

1.3.4 Signature Based IDS

Anti-virus software and SIDS function similarly. It searches a network for actions that are known to be harmful (Subba et al. 2016). SIDS similarly lacks the ability to identify emerging dangers. A new threat may take some time to be identified before SIDS actuallydetects it on a network.

1.3.5 Anomaly Based IDS

A functional baseline is created in anomaly-based IDS to depict what regular network activity should look like (Amouri et al. 2018). To ascertain if the activity is typical, the baseline is compared to samples of the network traffic. There is no assurance that hackers won't meddle with the system, even with the variety of IDS kinds that are available. The two most significant flaws are the update delay and the speed drop brought on the internal traffic monitoring. IDS's high FARs (False Alarm rates) are another issue.

1.3.6 Wireless

IDS in wireless examines network traffic while evaluating networking protocols to look for any potentially suspicious protocol-related behaviour. It is unable to detect this kind of behavior in wireless network traffic that is sent via application/higher-layer network protocols (TCP, UDP). Although it is often used to monitor a company's wireless network, it may also be used in places where unlawful wireless networking takes place.

1.3.7 Network Behavior Analysis (NBA)

NBA examines network traffic for identifying threats including Distributed Denial of Service (DDoS) attacks, specialized malwares (worms, backdoors), and policy violations that result in odd traffic patterns. (client systems giving network services to other clients). NBA systems are used to monitor network traffic both inside an organization's walls and between its internal networks.

1.4 INTRUSION DETECTION SYSTEM REQUIREMENTS

1.4.1 Information Required for Detection

Three types of data needed for identification are as follows (Anwar et al. 2017):

- System information: AMI device firmware/software integrity, clock synchronization, and health information from the meter and gateways (CPU, battery use).

- Network information: Rate of network collisions, the time it takes for a node to respond, packet loss, traffic volume, overall health, integrity of the routing table, and relationships between physical addresses and node identities.

- Policy information: Route updates, approved firmware upgrades, permitted AMI devices, permitted traffic patterns, and permitted AMI protocols.

Designing a complete and affordable monitoring system requires knowledge of how to map between assaults and the data needed to identify them. From a cost perspective, relying on attack manifestations at other system locations rather than routers for detection is a better strategy. In IDSs, events in computer systems or networks are monitored and checked for signs of possible issues. Traditional IDS components are (Zarpelão et al. 2017):

- Agents and sensors to track and analyze activities.

- A management server that monitors sensors and agents and combines the data they have gathered.

- A database server for IDS data production.

- A console with a user interface that allows system status checks, alarm monitoring, event investigation, and system configuration.

There are two primary reasons for the difference between these detecting methods. To begin, an IDS that is based on signatures utilizes a blacklist method, while an IDS that is based on anomalies and specifications uses a white list approach. A basic knowledge of harmful activity is required for a blacklist strategy, but a white list technique requires training for the system and the determination of its typical or appropriate behavior. The level of comprehension that is necessary for each strategy is a second key distinction. Although signature-based and anomaly-based intruder detecting systems are identical category because they monitor activity at a low level, specification-based intrusion detection systems need a high level and a complete grasp of the behavior that is being observed. Intruder detection system (IDS) dependability against intentional assaults and inadvertent failures is a second criterion, in addition to scalability. A system must continue to function even in the event that a subset of its sensors or even the management server is hacked or unavailable.

A computer system need to protect its users' privacy and safeguard itself against threats causing widespread denial of service. However, as a result of greater connectedness (particularly on the internet), as well as the huge spectrum of financial opportunities that are opening up, an increasing number of systems are being targeted by intruders, as shown in figure 1.4. These aim to take advantage of vulnerabilities in the operating system and in application applications, which may result in big events such as the Internet Worm issue that occurred in 1988.

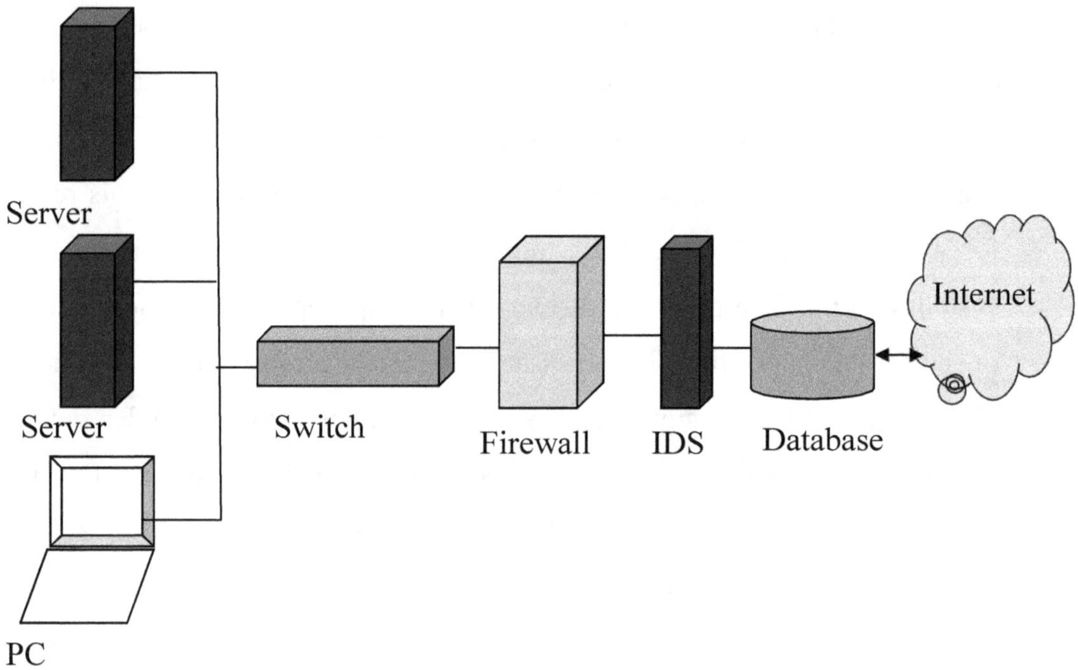

Figure 1.4 Intrusion Detection Systems

Subversion attempts can be handled in two ways. Building a system that is impenetrable by outsiders is one strategy to combat subversion (Yang 2016).

- IDS need to gain knowledge from its previous encounters and enhance its detection skills throughout the course of time. A self-tuning ID will learn from false alarms under the guidance of system administrators at first, and eventually on its own.

- Attack signatures should be readily and often added to IDS when new security bulletins, security patches, and protection flaws are found.

- System administrators need decision support tools to react to assaults. IDS should guarantee automatic remedial action in addition to detecting aberrant occurrences.

- The Intrusion Detection System (IDS) has to execute data fusion and interpret information from diverse and dispersed data sources, such as firewalls, routers, and switches. IDS should be able to interface with hardware-based devices because real-time monitoring requirements are forcing networked-based solutions to move toward reconfigurable hardware devices that can download new features.

- In order to handle the information obtained by data fusion methods, data reduction technologies are required by IDS. Tools for data mining allow statistical analysis tools to be conducted on archival data, which supports strategies for anomalous identification.

- An automatic reaction should be provided by IDS in the event of suspicious behavior.

- System administrators have a difficult time diagnosing issues and taking action to prevent the harm caused by intruders due to the rapid changes in light of the circumstances pertaining to the network and the limited experience of network administrators.

- This must be performed to have the ability to identify and respond to coordinated and widespread assaults. Assaults that are coordinated against a network will guarantee that a bigger number of troops are marshaled and that more and different attacks are launched against one target. These assaults may be variations of established attacks, can evolve quickly, and can be carried out with little financial investment by the attackers.

Denning and Neumann suggested that a comprehensive security plan for computer systems should include the use of efficient identification procedures. They came up with four reasons why identifying information should be used inside a framework for safe computing: 1. Existing computer systems include security defects that leave them open to attack, but these faults are difficult to locate and difficult to fix for a variety of technical and financial reasons. 2. Due to application and financial concerns, it is not possible to simply replace older systems that have security problems with newer systems that provide a higher level of protection. 3. It is not feasible to develop systems that are entirely safe. 4. Even systems that are very safe compromised by the improper usage of authorized users.

The currently deployed IDS operate on four presumptions about the systems they are intended to defend:

- Activities carried out by authorized and illegal users of the system may be watched.

- It is feasible to recognize behaviors that are indicators of an assault on a system.

- The information collected by IDS may be utilized in order to enhance the network's security level.

- The capability of an IDS system to do real-time analysis of an assault is the fourth feature that should be sought in an intrusion detection system. This would make it possible for the ID mechanism to lessen the harm brought on by an assault.

Utilizing this in an effective manner, is perhaps the single most challenging goal that IDS must accomplish.

1.4.2 Derived IDS Requirements

The identification of software needs for mobile agent software that is intended to detect FTP SITE EXEC intrusion was supported by software fault trees that were engaged in the intrusion (Moreaux et al. 2016). Examination of the penetration sub tree indicates that it is possible to identify an FTP SITE EXEC assault on software.

- Countermeasures for the FTP SITE EXEC: IDS may monitor PASS instructions in an FTP connection for data that does not reflect a legitimate sequence of printable characters thanks to derived requirements-based intrusion. In other words, an incorrect character sequence that contains more characters than the maximum permitted by the password size or a password that contains characters that cannot be printed constitutes an event in any minimum cut set.

1.5 INTRUSION ATTACKS

The great challenge lies in securing wireless ad-hoc networks. The first step is to study and understand possible form of attacks in order to develop secure solutions. Information must be sent securely, which depends on communication security in MANET. When compared to wired networks, MANET is more susceptible to digital/cyberattacks if it has a common wireless medium but no central coordination mechanism.

MANETs are vulnerable to several assaults. These assaults may be divided into two categories:

- External Attack: It is the attack that happens outside the network. Due to this attack, services are restricted due to the node by sending false routing information

- Internal Attack: Internal attacks are those which are caused from compromised nodes throughout the network. During this assault, a malware node acts as original node by using unauthorized rights. This attack has the ability to examine network activity between other nodes by looking at traffic between those nodes.

1.5.1 Types of Intrusion Attacks

Different forms of intruder assaults exist which are discussed as follows (Park et al. 2018):

Denial of Service (DoS)

DoS attack is one which tries to fully utilize the entire network. The services will be unavailable to authorized user if the attack succeeds. Generally, radio signal jamming and battery exhaustion method are used to accomplish the attack.

Eavesdropping

Eavesdropping is a kind of passively assault when the confidential information to be transmitted are observed by the node (Wiese et al. 2016). Additionally, a malignant node might use this data to retrieve confidential data, such a position, a public key, a private key, a password, etc.

Routing Attacks

The malignant node employs the following technique to access the objective routing service which is considered to be the most important service in networks (Apostolaki et al. 2017). There exist two types of routing attack. The first one deals with attacking the routing protocol in which it blocks the routing information propagation and second one deals with assault on the delivery or routing system for packets which disturbs the packet delivery against a predefined path.

Wormhole Attack

The packets are taken from where they were received by the attacker at one point in the network and sent to where they were originally received at another point in the network (Amish &Vaghela 2016). From that vantage point, this activity is performed several times inside the network. Because control messages are tunneled as part of this assault, routing information is disrupted. Wormhole refers to this passageway that connects two separate clouding assaults.

Replay Attack

In this attack, valid data are continuously retransmitted so that network routing traffic are injected which has been obtained previously. It mainly concentrates on routes disrupting but it is also used to weaken the poorly designed security solutions.

Jamming

In jamming, the frequency upon arrival at the last node, the signal is monitored from the sender along with the monitoring of wireless medium

(Deka et al. 2016). By this information, the signal is transmitted on the same frequency in order to make error free receptor.

Man-in-the-middle attack

During this assault, information that was sent between the sender and the recipient was intercepted and sniffed between the nodes. By using this information, miscommunication is initiated between the sender and receiver (Rahim 2017).

Gray-hole attack

Here messages may be dropped, due to which there will be misbehavior in routing, hence called routing misbehavior attack (Gurung& Chauhan 2018). There are two phases in this attack in which a valid route is presented by the node itself in first phase. The packets may be dropped with a certain probability by the nodes in the second phase.

Black-hole attacks

Attacks known as black holes occur when a malicious node fails to send any message that has arrived at the node to its intended recipient once the message reaches the node. Here, the effected node purposely drops all incoming packets (Rao et al. 2018).

Sinkhole Attacks

Sinkhole attacks are almost same as black-hole attack (Rehman et al. 2019). The difference is that it advertises to have the best path to various destinations, thereby creating more data traffic. It serves as a basis for other attacks.

Sybil attack

Sybil attack is one in which malicious node may imitate a node which in turn affects the routing protocols by repeating it (Jan et al. 2018). It also damages the integrity of the data, which the distributed method seeks to accomplish, as well as the security and the usage of the resources. The Sybil attack is very widespread in storage, routing mechanisms, the distribution of air resources, and the detection of inappropriate conduct.

1.6 TYPES OF INTRUSION DETECTION TECHNIQUES

There are three types of Intrusion Detection mechanisms (Shanthi&Rajan 2016). These are Anomaly based, Signature based and Specification based Intrusion Detection Methods.

1.6.1 Anomaly Based Intrusion Detection Technique

Anomaly refers to the abnormal peculiarities or exceptions in the data pattern which occurs randomly (Aljawarneh et al. 2018). The methodology for abnormality identification is created in a manner that the patterns which are abnormal are uncovered and other individuals are marked as intrusions. Static and dynamic detectors are used to identify anomalies. A static anomaly detector is one that always observes the same portion of the monitored system. System data and system code make up the two components that make up the static section. The portion which is static is noted as a binary bit. If the static portion is altered from its original form, it indicates that the intruder has intruded the portion of the apparatus. The system's behaviour is described in terms of the sequence of various occurrences in a dynamic anomaly detector. IDS, for instance, uses audit data generated by the operating system to specify the events of interest. In this instance, the action can only be seen if the OS creates audit records and the events take place in a certain order. Alarms may sound if ambiguous activity is deemed unusual, alerting the system administrators.

The ability of anomaly detection to identify unanticipated assaults or undiscovered weaknesses is its key benefit. This detection approach is very helpful for identifying threats like protocol abuse, service port abuse, denial of service based on manipulated payloads or volume, buffer overflow, and other application payload anomalies. The disadvantages of Anomaly detection method is its difficulty to configure because complete knowledge about expected behavior has to be set up and the production of high false positive alerts. Several Techniques exist to implement anomaly detection. They differ based on the representation of the normal profile and estimating the differences between the observed characteristics and the normal behavioral characteristics. Normally, statistics and neural networks are applied for implementation.

Statistical Models

The result is presented in the form of a statistical value by the statistical model. There are two distinct categories of statistical models, and these categories are

- Operational Model (or) Threshold Metric: Consider a scenario in which a user tries to log in but is unsuccessful at times; this will cause the alarm to sound. The lowest and maximum values that may be used are 0 and n, respectively. This kind of action which regulates the alarm is termed as Operational Model (or) Threshold Metric.

- Markov Process or Marker Model: Here fixed time interval is used to inspect the system. For example, when the probability of the state is low, the behavior is considered as anomaly.

Cognition Models

- Finite State Machine (FSM): FSM or finite automations are representations of models that imitate states, transitions, and operations of systems. A state consists of nothing more than information regarding its previous existence. An entrance action, an exit action, or a transition action is an example of a sort of action. An action is defined as anything that defines an activity that is going to be carried out at a certain time.

- Description Scripts: Attacks on computers and networks are often characterized by the use of scripting languages. Every scripting language has the ability to check the order in which certain actions take place in order to identify any irregularities.

1.6.2 Signature Based Intrusion Detection

The identification of an intrusion using signature-based intrusion detection is accomplished by consulting a database that contains information on previously discovered vulnerabilities and assaults. That is, in the database, the dataset contains many cases, and labelling is done for the data either as normal or intrusive (Wang et al. 2018). This data set labeling is done by using machine learning algorithms. Signature is maintained automatically for identifying and detecting the intruder. This technique is also termed as Misuse detection technique. Misuse detection technique is created automatically which is more complicated and is also accurate than the manual technique.

The factors such as robustness and seriousness of a signature are used in alarm or notification enabling signal within the system and it is sent to the right authorities at the right time. Misuse-based identification has a number of drawbacks, but the biggest one is that it is impossible to protect against all conceivable forms of assaults and to create a signature. Besides new attacks are tough to be predicted.

Techniques used in misuse detection:

- Expression matching: Expression comparison is the least complicated and most straightforward form of all abuse detection techniques. In this, exploration of a stream of events is done like log entries in order to match the exact pattern.

- State transition analysis: The network's state or its internal transitions serve as the basis for this concept. Transitions may be produced by applying network events to a finite state system. Once it reaches the final state it indicates that an attack has occurred.

1.6.3 Specification Based Intrusion Detection

This is a novel intruder detecting method that incorporates the characteristics and advantages of both, anomaly and misuse. This technique uses specifications which are manually developed and has the least possibilities for FARs. The specification based method monitors program behaviors and analyzes it for deviations in the specifications registered for that program behavior. It is also capable to report new and unforeseen attacks and vulnerabilities (Esquivel-Vargas et al. 2017).

1.7 PROBLEM DEFINITION

In the existing work, Mean Shift Clustering based Intrusion Detection is introduced for secured data transmission. However, the problems found in the existing research work are listed below:

- The main drawback of existing research work is increased time complexity where there will not be initialized number of clusters. In the existing work, smaller deviation in the data point will also be considered as abnormal data.

- Weighted SVM algorithm utilized in the existing work would lead to more computational overhead and reduced accuracy with more/a larger collection of resourcepoints.

- The existing research works will not support many types of assaults are occurring on the network.

- Existing research work doesn't concentrate on the privacy concerns of users who are attempting to utilize the wireless sensor network for data transmission.

1.8 OBJECTIVE

The primary goal of the research methodology is listed below:

- To introduce the methodology which can significantly minimize the computing burden of intruder identification and guarantee the accurate attack detection rate.

- To implement the methodology which can detect all kinds of attacks happening on the network.

- To introduce the methodology which can ensure the privacy attributes of the research methodology.

1.9 RESEARCH CONTRIBUTION

Following is a list of this technical work's main contributions: Introducing the methodology Traffic Variation based Intrusion Detection System (TV-IDS) for ensuring the accurate intrusion detection. Implementing the Computation Overhead Reduced Fragmentation Intrusion Detection System (CORF-IDS) to guarantee the secured and overhead reduced data transmission. Designing and implementing the methodology called Computation Overhead Reduced Privacy Concerned Data Transmission (COR-PCDT) for ensuring the privacy and security aware data transmission.

1.10 ORGANIZATION OF THE THESIS

Following are the parts that make up the thesis's structure:

Chapter 1 presents an introduction to Intrusion Detection Systems (IDS) and its types followed by the objective of the research work.

Chapter 2 presents a discussion of the many previous research papers that are pertinent to the work that is given in this thesis.

Chapter 3 deals with detailed study among the suggested Traffic Variation Based Intrusion Detection System which has resulted in improved overall security and results are presented.

Chapter 4 describes a novel approach of Computation Overhead Reduced Fragmentation Intrusion Detection System which is proposed to increase the PDRs and reduce false positive rates.

Chapter 5 discusses on the proposed Computation Overhead Reduced Privacy Concerned Data Transmission

Chapter 6 concludes the contributions and findings in addition to suggestions for future enhancement.

1.11 SUMMARY

This chapter provides discussion of wireless sensor network and its security issues has been discussed. This chapter provides the detailed introduction about the intruder detecting device and its function in the wireless sensor network's security. This chapter also provides the discussion about the various methodologies that attempt in order to identify the intrusion assaults that are now taking place on the network. In addition to discussing the function of detecting intrusions in wireless sensor networks, this chapter delves into the many kinds the use intruder detecting devices, various kinds of cyberattacks that are the focus of this study. Overall, this chapter provides the detailed overview of wireless sensor network, security issues, need of IDS and its role in providing security factors.

CHAPTER 2

LITERATURE REVIEW

2.1 INTRODUCTION

The Wireless Sensor Network (WSN) is a system of self-contained, autonomous sensors that keep an eye on physically parameters while having limitations on its battery life, memory capacity, and computational power. Sensor nodes on WSN installations are susceptible to a number of threats, including sinkhole, wormhole, selective forward, sybil, and clone assaults as well as scattered Denial of Service (DoS) threats. Designing detection techniques against DoS assaults entails a variety of risky issues and challenges, and DDoS assaults have increased since a crucial research topic in sensor network security.

An outline of the is provided in this chapter fundamentals, difficulties, and security objectives in WSNs as well as the many forms of attacks that can be detected in WSNs and cause data loss, data compromise, and node energy consumption. This chapter offers an overview of the various assaults in WSN, their detection, and prevention.

Review on the various attack types, strategies for identification and avoidance in wireless sensor networks is divided into four categories: i)security concerns in wireless sensor networks; (ii) identification of intrusions system; (iii) optimization algorithm in intrusion detection; and

(iv) firecol in intrusion detection system. These four approaches, which can address a wide range of attack detection and prevention issues, are discussed.

2.2 REVIEW ON SECURITY ISSUES IN WIRELESS SENSOR NETWORK

In order to identify wormhole assaults in WSN, Shahryari and Naji (Shahryari & Naji 2015) created a grouping algorithm-based intruder detecting system. The Modified Low Energy Adaptive Clustering Hierarchy (M-LEACH) protocol is the foundation for the clustering that is being done. Round is a term for the equal-length segments that make up time. There are four phases in each round: setup, member verification, Cluster Head (CH) routing, and steady state. Each cluster has a CH, as well as several nodes that are member nodes (non-CH). Only the cluster head receives the information from member nodes. The cluster leader must communicate the combined information to each cluster member. The cluster head, who is chosen based on a dynamic process, maintains the routing information. The advantage of protocol is that malicious nodes are identified during attack detection or attack prevention without the need for additional hardware or sophisticated calculations. In comparison to a network that is not under attack or that is, the protocol has been evaluated in terms of packet drop ratio, throughput, latency, and energy usage. The NS-2 simulator's simulation results are examined. The results of the simulation show that the protocol is practical and effective in boosting resistance to wormhole assaults.

Almomani et al. in their study considered popular hierarchical routing technique, Low Energy Adaptive Clustering Hierarchy (LEACH) and Artificial Neural Network (ANN) for detecting DoS attacks in WSN. Their method was used to accurately identify and categorize different DoS attacks including Blackholes, Grayholes, Flooding, and Scheduling. Their simulations on Network Simulator 2 (NS-2) used 23 characteristics. The gathered data set is known as WSN-DS was trained using ANN to recognize and categorize various DoS attacks. Their findings show improved IDS functionality with higher classification accuracy rates. The WEKA toolset was utilized in conjunction with the 10-Fold Cross Validation and Holdout processes. The best results were obtained using 10-Fold Cross Validation with a single hidden layer. The classification accuracy of the Blackhole, Flooding, Scheduling, and Grayhole assaults, in addition to the ordinary situation (without attacks), was 92.8%, 99.4%, 92.2%, 75.6%, and 99.8%, respectively.

Abnormal Sensor Detection Accuracy Rivest-Shamir-Adleman (ASDARSA) was proposed by Fotohi et al. (Fotohi et al. 2022) for the detection of DoS assaults in WSN. To combat DoS attacks and lower energy consumption, the ASDA-RSA approach is used. There are two phases to the ASDA-RSA schema, which improves security in WSNs. Once the right CHs were chosen in the first phase, authentication mechanisms, interlock protocols, RSA cryptographic methodologies, and grouping strategies based on energies and distance s were e utilized to avoid DoS assaults in the second phase. Simulations on NS2 evaluated their ASDA-RSA method where findings showed that average throughputs, PDRs (Packet Delivery Ratios), network lifetimes, detection ratios, and average residual energies of WSN networks improved.

For the purpose of detecting replication attacks in WSN, (Cheng et al. 2015) proposed enhanced Low Energy Adaptive Clustering Hierarchy (NI-LEACH) where ideal group counts and residual energies of nodes were considered. NI-LEACH approach shrunk group sizes. Additionally, to significantly lower the likelihood of data modification, add monitor nodes to the network and design an intruder detection mechanism to identify duplicate attempts. Simulations results show how simple and effective the recommended approach is. A high degree of probability may be used to identify an intruder while achieving throughput that is close to optimum. The resistance of the network to clone node attacks is significantly enhanced.

The False Node Exclusion DoS (FNEDoS) method was introduced by Abdulqader AL-Shaihk and Hassanpour (Al-Shaihk & Hassanpour 2019) as a result of jamming attack detection in WSN. DoS attack caused by additional communications from the cluster head that lowers network performance. FEDOS method restriction prevents innocent nodes from supporting reports broadcast by the cluster head. A method to find and use alternate safe channels for sending the endorsements of the nodes under assault is part of the upgrade. The suggested approach entails creating an algorithm that can avoid an attacked path in favour of a safe one that is controlled by the group head to lessen the False Node Excluding DoS brought on by an attack using delaying. The FEDoS method's false-excluding issue is a direct result of the proof endorsements' delayed delivery as a result of ongoing jamming assaults. To avoid omitting functional nodes from future report endorsements, this has to be improved. With arbitrary study examples, Empirical comparisons between their proposed and other related methods found in literature were made. In the case of single nodes, the suggested method yields a complete restoration of the affected node, and results are improved when the attack targets a cluster of nodes close to each other.

Saghar et al. (2016) proposed Robust Formally Analyzed protocol for WirEless Sensor Networks Deployment (RAEED) with the aim of identifying DoS attacks in WSN. The three main phases of the RAEED proposed protocol are Key Setup Phase (KSP), Route Setup Phase (RSP), and Data Forward Phase (DFP), which are further divided into various sub-phases. The two main KSP stages are Key Exchange Phase (KEP) and Bidirectional Verification Phase (BVP). During the Route Setup Phase, verified 1-hop and 2-hop neighbour node IDs are swapped (RSP). Because they were found in the KSP, it should be noted that these neighbours are validated. Data Forward Phase enables Nodes to do neighbourhood ranking and local monitoring (DFP). The rating is based on the data forwarding abilities of the neighbours. DFP must be used to defeat assaults like the black hole, grey hole, jamming, misbehaviour (selfishness), and framing attacks. Finally, the results of formal approaches have been validated by computer simulations and actual use on McaZ motes.

To combat wormhole attacks in WSN, Tiwari et al. (2015) developed the Modified Hop Count Analysis Algorithm (MHCAA). MHCAA suggested methods for identifying and avoiding wormhole attacks, especially hop-count monitoring and attack identification depending on specifications. Modeling wormhole attacks has been used to assess how well the offered techniques function. Security approach simulations make it possible to choose an appropriate security solution for routing protocols and understand how to put these plans into practise in hostile and corrupted environments. Simulation results demonstrate that the recommended solutions perform better when throughput, average end-to-end latency, and PDRs rise. In the situation under consideration, it is discovered that the modified Ad hoc On demand Distance Vector (AODV) performs better than AODV. Wormhole attacks can be recognised and prevented using the updated AODV. It improves the PDR in assault situations with a small throughput drop and an acceptable increase in end-to-end latency.

Geographic Routing to Multiple Sinks in Connected Wireless Sensor Networks Based on Multiple Sinks (GRPW-MuS) was developed by Sabri & El Kamoun (2016) to identify wormhole attacks in WSNs. GRPW-MuS used basic routing protocols to support WSN's mobile sinks. In order to lessen the amount of topology broadcast, the GRPW-MuS geographical routing protocol is designed with logical layers that are separated by multipoint relaying floods. Periodic HELLO packets are used by GRPW-MuS to locate neighbours. In particular, many WSN routing procedures and place-based wireless security systems are vulnerable to wormhole attacks, which pose a severe danger to WSN. Here, a trust model called GRPW-MuS-s is offered to handle this assault in GRPW-MuS. Data acquired using the OMNET++ simulator and the MiXiM platform show that the amount of false positives for wormhole identification in the neighbour discovery phase of the GRPW-MuS-s protocol is relatively low. While performing neighbour and route discovery, the GRPW-MuS protocol uses an average amount of energy at each node that is far less than the energy that is physically present at each node. The cost analysis demonstrates that the GRPW-MuS-s protocol is appropriate for the sensor network because each node only requires a tiny amount of memory use.

Support Vector Machine (SVM) and Radial Basis Function (RBF) were proposed by Kato & Klyuev (2014) for the identification of DDoS attacks in WSN. The DDoS attack patterns for each IP address and the data from the DDoS assault detecting platform were used to substantial amount of network communication packets. the difficulties in developing a DDoS assault detecting method that uses packets and important DDoS attack traits. These factors may have a significant positive impact on the creation of a DDoS assault monitoring system. Intelligent DDoS attack detection system to protect network services. The technology was created using machine learning methods after patterns of DDoS assaults were examined. Furthermore, a sizable number of network packets supplied by the Center for Applied Internet Data Analysis were studied, and certain important trends that influence the detecting system's effectiveness were discovered. Then a detection system was put into place using DDoS attack patterns. Its main component is an SVM with an RBF (Gaussian) kernel. Three different dataset types that use three and five attributes. The process for developing a DDoS assault detecting systems illustrates how an SVM detecting systems taught with the specified characteristics may reliably and correctly predict DDoS assaults. The detection technology is capable of properly identifying DDoS assaults.

For the purpose of detecting DDoS attacks in Software Defined Networking, Cui et al. (2016) created a Software Defined Anti-Distributed Denial of Service (SD-AntiDDoS) (SDN). There are four components that make up the SD-AntiDDoS mechanisms including detections of triggers, tracebacks, and mitigations for attacks. To combat DDoS attacks more rapidly and lessen the stress on controllers and switches, the trigger of the threat detecting technique is first presented. In the interim, a neural network-based DDoS attack detection technology is used to identify attacks. The proposal also includes an attack traceback technique that makes use of SDN's capabilities. A DDoS mitigation system that includes attack blocking and flow table cleaning is also in place. On the SDN testbed, the proposed methodology is assessed. According to experimental findings, the suggested system may detect attacks in less than one second and reliably pinpoint their origin. More crucially, it has the ability to stop an attack at its source and free up switches' occupied resources.

For the purpose of detecting DDoS assaults in WSNs built on SDN, Giotis et al. (2014) presented an OpenFlow (OF), sFlow, and entropy-based Detection and Classification of Anomalies. It is a scalable and effective approach for detecting and mitigating anomalies in SDN architectures. The owners and operators of networked resources may use flow statistics to identify anomalies brought on by large-scale harmful activities (usually powerful DDoS attacks) and to develop mitigation strategies against these dangers. First, show how the centralized control plane becomes overloaded during the gathering and processing of statistics, creating scalability problems. Second, using sFlow monitoring data, provide a modular design for separating the SDN control plane's data collection procedure. Report the experimental findings after comparing compared to native methods that use traditional flow table statistics, its efficiency. Using extensive actual network traffic statistics collected from a campus network at an institution, both solutions are assessed using an entropy-based methodology. The packet traces that were sent to hardware and software devices were used to test the flow-based data collection and related abnormality identification systems. Suggested sFlow-based method was compared with native methods, in terms of the overheads imposed on consumption of system resources. Finally, show that the protocol can successfully mitigate a network anomaly using flow table alterations once it has been spotted and identified.

Osanaiye et al. (2018) established exponentially weighed moving averages to identify DoS jamming assaults on WSNs (EWMA) using packet inter arrivals of packets collected from sensor nodes, EWMA was able to recognize irregular fluctuations in strengths of jammer attacks. Their jamming detection method, deployed on both CH and base stations to detect attacks on member nodes using packet's Inter-Arrival Time (IAT) metrics. This step-by-step method was proposed for detecting various types of jamming attacks. This metric is used to identify sudden changes in packet sequence brought on by jamming assaults when the EMWA algorithm is being employed. A trace-driven experiment using EWMA to determine differences in traffic flow in both non-jamming and jamming attack conditions demonstrated the effectiveness of the suggested approach. The three distinct jamming attack variants from the CRAWDAD dataset and a non-jamming trace were also utilized to assess EMWA. The proposed method may effectively and precisely identify jamming attacks in WSNs with little to no overhead, according to the results of a trace-driven simulation.

For the purpose of detecting sybil attacks in WSN, Sarigiannidis et al. (2015) suggested the Rule-based Anomaly Detection System (RADS). In order to protect themselves from the Sybil attack, a particularly dangerous type of assault, RADS restrains its attention. By causing disruptions in numerous networking protocols, sybil attacks have the potential to significantly reduce network performance and jeopardise security. Large-scale WSNs employ RADS, rule based anomaly detection systems to monitor or quickly spot Sybil assaults. The proposed expert system built on a distributed Ultra-WideBand (UWB) ranging based detection algorithm, handles anomaly detection tasks without the need for co-operation or data sharing across sensor nodes. Analytical evidence is provided to support the viability of the suggested approach, and RADS' effectiveness in revealing Sybil attacks has been thoroughly evaluated on both mathematical and numerical level. The findings demonstrate that RADS is a viable replacement for ADS in these kind of wireless networks due to its high identification efficiency and low FARs .

To identify threats that are selectively sent in WSN, Ren et al. (2016) proposed the Channel-aware Reputation System with Adaptive detection threshold (CRS-A). Based on the discrepancy between the observed packet loss and the expected normal loss, CRS-A assesses the data transmission methods used by sensor nodes. The ideal threshold for forwarding evaluation that may be modified to the time-varying channel state and the predicted danger likelihood of compromised nodes may theoretically be determined in order to improve the identification reliability of CRS-A. An attack-tolerant data giving mechanism is also designed to interact with CRS-A in order to persuade compromised nodes to comply with forwarding and increase the network's data delivery ratio. Numerous simulation findings show that the attack-tolerant data forwarding strategy may greatly increase the network's data delivery ratio while CRS-A could recognize compromised sensor nodes accurately and detect selective forward assaults.

For the purpose of detecting threats in WSN, Duan et al. (2014) created the Trust-aware Secure Routing Framework (TSRF). Lightweight and highly capable of fending off multiple attacks, the TSRF. First, examine the characteristics of typical attacks on trust-aware routing techniques that adhere to the privacy standards of the WSNs' routing protocols. Then, depending on the findings of the analysis, specific trust extraction and calculation techniques are suggested. Finally, design presents an optimized routing algorithm using the use of both trust metrics and quality of service measurements as routing metrics. The simulation findings demonstrated TSRF may improve network throughput and has a wide range of applications. under the presumption of security assurance, particularly in congested networks, when compared to various existing trust-ware techniques. Additionally, demonstrate using simulations that TSRF is capable of achieving both expected security and high efficacy appropriate for WSN-based networks.

A Quality of Protection Modeling Language (QoP-ML) was proposed by Mazur et al. (2016) for the detection of DDoS, flooding assaults in WSN. A network for analyzing the health of structures that has been disrupted by one of the most prevalent DDoS attack types, the flooding assault, was developed by QoP-ML. Explore the reach of the flood-based DDoS attack issue through a series of simulations, evaluating the network's performance and lifetime under the attack conditions. QoP-ML, a wide range of network setups, characteristics, attack choices, and scenarios might be examined. It is possible to carefully analyse and characterise how to offer DoS defenses at the lastcost, ensuring both the established security objectives and network connection availability during the attack. We were able to recognise a brand-new DDoS attack known as the Delayed Distributed Denial of Service, or DDDoS attack, thanks to the findings of the meticulously carried out multilevel analysis. Investigation of DDoS attacks using a tiered methodology demonstrated the importance of consider numerous variables at once while assessing threatened environments in order to not miss any crucial details.

A Fast and Flexible Unsupervised Clustering Algorithm (FFUCA) was created by Fouchal et al. (2015) for the detection of DoS attacks in WSN. Threats caused by a lack of rest are of particular attention, including those carried out by hostile nodes that employ flooding. The foundation of this strategy is WSN clustering. In order to get the appropriate degree of resolution, it involves continually grouping sensors. The approach utilized two different clustering methods, WSN's LEACH and FFUCA universal clustering strategy, based on ultra-metric characteristics. The behaviour of the two algorithms were also detailed and providing numerical evidence of the effectiveness of FFUCA algorithm-based recursive clustering.

Table 2.1 Inference of security issues in wireless sensor network

S.NO	AUTHOR NAME	METHOD NAME	ADVANTAGES	DISADVANTAGES
1	Shahryari and Naji	clustering method	improving resilience against wormhole attacks	It is does not consume the high energy
2	Almomani et al.	Low Energy Adaptive Clustering Hierarchy (LEACH) and Artificial Neural Network (ANN)	higher classification accuracy rate	Not focus as wormhole or sybil attack

Table 2.1 (Continued)

3	Fotohi et al.	Abnormal Sensor Detection Accuracy Rivest-Shamir-Adleman (ASDA-RSA)	decrease the amount of energy used and lengthen the network lifespan	Not suitable for meta-heuristic algorithms
4	Cheng et al.	improved Low Energy Adaptive Clustering Hierarchy (NI-LEACH)	Attacks from clone nodes are far more effective	Cluster heads are distributed erratically and unevenly
5	Abdulqader AL-Shaihk and Hassanpour	clustering-based for False Node Exclusion DoS (FNEDoS)	improved jamming attack detection	Not focused on reduce power consumption
6	Saghar et al.	Robust formally Analysed protocol for wirEless sEnsor networks Deployment (RAEED)	avoid sinkhole attack	Not focused on wormhole and INA attacker
7	Tiwari et al.	Modified Hop Count Analysis Algorithm (MHCAA)	identify and stop wormhole attacks, enhance PDR, reduce throughput, and lengthen end-to-end latency	The route finding procedure may result in the loss of the shortest path owing to traffic.
8	Sabri and El Kamoun	Geographic Routing to Multiple Sinks in connected wireless sensor networks based on Multiple Sinks (GRPW-MuS)	identification of wormhole assaults	how to protect the delivery of a trustworthy information
9	Kato and Klyuev	SVM and Radial Basis Function (RBF)	DDoS detecting attacks with high accuracy	performs poorly when there is greater distortion in the data collection

Table 2.1 (Continued)

10	Cui et al.	Software Defined Anti-Distributed Denial of Service (SD-AntiDDoS)	Minimize the network demand, CPU burden, and reaction time	Not suitable for larger dataset
11	Giotis et al.	OpenFlow (OF), sFlow and Entropy-based Detection and Classification	anomaly detection accuracy	Studying and experimenting with inter-domain OF controllers is not a concentrated endeavor.
12	Osanaiye et al.	Exponentially Weighted Moving Average (EWMA)	detect DDoS attacks with high accuracy	Not focused on real-world environment
13	Sarigiannidis et al.	Rule-based Anomaly Detection System (RADS)	high Sybil attack detection accuracy and low FARs	not be able to identify other security concerns like wormhole, sinkhole, and hello flood assaults
14	Ren et al.	Channel-aware Reputation System with Adaptive detection threshold (CRS-A)	effectively identify selectively transmitting assaults, raise the network's data delivery efficiency	The usual packet loss rate is more variable and challenging to calculate
15	Duan et al.	Trust-aware Secure Routing Framework (TSRF)	improve the performance of the network	Focused distributed attack detecting solutions for WSNs are not included
16	Mazur et al.	Quality of Protection Modeling Language (QoP-ML)	issue with flood-based DDoS attacks, evaluating the network's efficiency and lifespan	Not suitable for complex Internet of Things (IoT) network architecture

Table 2.1 (Continued)

17	Fouchal et al.	Fast and Flexible Unsupervised Clustering Algorithm (FFUCA)	The multicast's overall bandwidth usage is kept to a minimum	Larger datasets are not appropriate for it

2.3 REVIEW ON INTRUSION DETECTION SYSTEM

Shamshirband et al. (2014) built a Game-based Fuzzy Q-learning (G-FQL) system for WSN DDoS attack detection. Cooperative G-FQL is a game-theoretic technique. G-FQL integrates Q-learning and game theory in WSNs. Attacker, base station, and sink nodes play this strategic game. When a victim node in the network exceeds a specified WSN alarm event threshold, the game begins. By leveraging game theory, the recommended model allows sink node and base station to make logical decisions in counter-attack circumstances. NS-2 was used to simulate LEACH to test the proposed model. The model was compared to other soft computing techniques including fuzzy logic controllers, Q-learning, and fuzzy Q-learning, to emphasize its utility and feasibility. Attack detection and defensive precision are better with the suggested model than with earlier machine learning methods. In terms of defensive rate, the suggested model outperforms the Markovian game theoretic model.

Jianjian et al. (2018) presented IABRBFSVM for DoS attack detection in IDS (IDS). Using an updated AdaBoost-RBFSVM, a DoS attack against WSNs is built. After training, RBF-SVM becomes AdaBoost poor classifier. The use of IABRBFSVM due to the parameter's impact on RBF-SVM and model's training errors on AdaBoost weight smoothing was of simple design, quick computations, and high recognition rates. The eigen spaces of the attacks suggested subsequent analysis of DoS assaults for creating IDSs. By detecting and deleting dangerous nodes, the proposed IDSs may enhance network detection rates, packet delivery rates, transmission delays, and energy consumption analyses.

Ahmad et al. (2021) presented LEACH) and ANN. IDSs which is equipped to locate a wide variety of possible dangers in WSN for the aim of detecting DoS attacks on wireless sensor networks. A customised dataset for underwater smart WSNs that may be separated into four different types of DoS attacks is included in the proposal (Blackhole, Grayhole, Flooding and Scheduling attacks). Since the LEACH protocol is widely used in WSN, it was chosen for the experiment. Vector-based forwarding offers a scalable routing technique for the installation of wireless underwater sensor networks. Using the NS2 networking simulation model, a method for gathering network traffic and creating the dataset has been provided. The dataset was trained using ANN in order to categorise it into several DoS attacks. With the use of the suggested dataset, the experimental technique shown here provides good classification rates and accuracy for mentioning attacks. This method could also be used for assessing Sybil/Wormhole attacks of the data link layers.

In order to detect routing assaults on WSN, Maleh and Ezzati (2015) a SVM was first used for intrusion detection. Each of the several groupings of the sensor array's units has a ClusterHead. A cluster-based design follows (CH). CH is used to cut down on energy consumption, reduce network data volume, and extend network life. This is accomplished by choosing one to act as the group leader (CH), who sends packets (data aggregated) to the base station (BS) rather than requiring all nodes to communicate their collected data to a distant location (BS). WSN are set up and arranged in a hierarchical routing architecture using cluster-based protocols. The outputs of rule-based and SVM-based anomaly detection are combined in a decision-making model. It establishes whether an incursion has taken place and categorises the different types of attacks. The administrator is then informed of the decision making model's output for oversight. The suggested intruder detecting approach makes use of SVM and signature models in order to identify malicious behaviour and offer a global, light-weight IDS in a cluster-based architecture. The majority of routing attacks can be found and avoided by the suggested model.

Guo et al. (2017) created Algebra for Wireless Mesh Networks (AWN) in Multi-Protocol Oriented Middleware-level Intrusion Detection (MP-MID) to recognise various WSN threats. For each WSN routing system, the proposed MP-MID can produce every known attack type, and all of them may be identified using automatically generated rules. By utilising the Process AWN language, formalise the routing protocol by introducing the idea of attack sites to detect all types of attacks. Co-sentences that explain the attack characteristics in the protocol are produced by fusing attack points with defined protocol in AWN. Using co-sentence-based programme slicing methods, all known assault types may be recognised. Depending on the nature of the primary attack type variables, MP-MID can deliver misused-based detection or anomaly-based detection. The On-Demand Ad hoc Distance Vector (ADOV) case study demonstrates how the system created all types of attacks and outperformed prior efforts. Experimental findings support the premise that produced detection approaches possess a high degree of detecting reliability. The MP-MID approach could be utilised as a versatile and all-encompassing tool to efficiently assess and detect various multi-protocol attack types in WSN.

Spectral Clustering and Deep Neural Network (SCDNN) was introduced by Ma et al. (2016) as a method for use in intrusion detection for anomalous attacks detections of WSNs. This tool was created specifically for use with WSN. Spectral Clustering (SC) and Deep Neural Network (DNN) methods are used in hybrid Spectral Clustering Deep Neural Network (SCDNN). Starting off, the dataset is separated into k subgroups using cluster centres, same as was done in SC, depending on how similar its individual samples are to one another. The technique of a deep neural network is then applied to the task of intrusion detection. Distances between data points in training and testing sets were computed based on similarities. To evaluate the model's performance, six datasets from the KDD-Cup99 and NSL-KDD competitions as well as one dataset from a sensor network were used. The outcomes of these tests show that the SCDNN classifier not only surpasses other models in terms of detection accuracy and the types of aberrant assaults that are recognised, such as the Bayes tree, SVM, Random Forest, and Back Propagation Neural Network models. Additionally, it offers a useful tool for research, notably work on the identification of attackers in huge networks.

To evaluate the model's performance, six datasets from the KDD-Cup99 and NSL-KDD competitions as well as one dataset from a sensor network were used. The outcomes of these tests show that the SCDNN classifier not only surpasses other models in terms of detection accuracy and the types of aberrant assaults that are recognised, such as the Bayes tree, Support Vector Machine, Random Forest, and Back Propagation Neural Network models. Additionally, it offers a useful tool for research, notably work on the identification of attackers in huge networks. The ICA is improved by a density-based clustering approach for handling noise and creating variable cluster shapes. The Fuzzy Logic Controller (FLC) adjusts to imperialistic competition by changing the fuzzy rules to take into account any errors in the worst imperialist action selection strategy. The proposed method aims to increase the accuracy of malicious detection. A publicly accessible dataset of exact measurements obtained from sensors deployed at the Intel Berkeley Research Lab is used to assess D-FICCA. Its performance is evaluated in comparison to those of earlier empirical methods like K-MICA,

K-mean, and DBSCAN. The outcomes show that in terms of detecting accuracy and grouping grade 0.99, the suggested framework performs better than the existing alternatives.

In order to detect DDoS assaults for WSN, Cepheli et al. (2016) suggested a Hybrid Intrusion Detection System (H-IDS) that uses Gaussian Mixture Models (GMMs). The results of both detectors are combined in the proposed detection system to increase overall detection accuracy. The suggested detecting system integrates both anomaly-based and signature-based detecting techniques, but does so individually. H-IDS is created using multidimensional GMMs from a training dataset, whereas SNORT is used to create the signature-based detector. Additionally, create a node called the Hybrid Detection Engine (HDE) to manage and assess the outputs of these detectors. By utilizing two detectors individually yet in concert, the suggested H-IDS improved lowered the detecting latency and improved overall DDoS threat detecting efficiency. The recommended H-IDS may be used as an IDS solution module or as a stand-alone DDoS detecting system. Throughout a vulnerability test, utilise the widely-used DARPA 2000 dataset and a dataset given by a commercial bank in Turkey to evaluate the detection performance of the suggested hybrid detector. True Positive Rate (TPR) for the commercial bank dataset with the H-IDS is 99.9% and for DARPA is 92.1%. Finally, DARPA and commercial bank datasets were employed to evaluate the suggested hybrid system's detecting efficiency, and the results showed that it performs better than systems based on non-hybrid detection.

SVM and Radial Basis Function (RBF) for intrusion detection for DDoS attacks detection WSN were developed by Kato & Klyuev (2014). The recommended strategy is to develop an intelligent DDoS attack detection system by detecting their patterns via network packet analysis and researching them using machine learning methods. DDoS attack detection method employing the IP address-specific DDoS assault patterns. DDoS attack detection system employs packets and key DDoS attack characteristics to identify attacks. The development of a DDoS attack detection system can benefit greatly from these aspects. After analysing the packets and determining the bytes per second using the time sequence, it was discovered that DDoS attacks primarily occur during two periods. In this study, The detection method was developed using SVM with the RBF (Gaussian) kernel after a substantial number of network packets from the Center for Applied Internet Data Analysis were analyzed. The detection technology is capable of properly identifying DDoS assaults.

In order to detect DoS attacks on WSNs, Riecker et al. (2013) introduced a linear regression in intrusion detection. The proposed system uses mobile agents to identify intrusions by monitoring the energy usage of the sensor nodes. It is compact and energy-efficient. Using a linear regression model, energy use is predicted. Additionally, none requires nodes to communicate with one another, monitor their surroundings, or provide audit data to a central location. Use a mobile agent instead that gathers energy statistics and alerts you if anything changes abruptly. It has been shown that using mobile agents for intrusion detection in WSN is feasible. The amount of energy used is an appropriate indicator for identifying DoS assaults. According to simulation studies, DoS assaults like floods can be determined with great precision and very little false positive data.

Hoyos Ll et al. (2016) developed an IDS SVM with the purpose of detecting DDoS attacks. The capture of network traffic, the filtering of HTTP headers, One method that is suggested for the detection of prototype DDoS attacks includes the normalisation of the data based on operational characteristics such as rate of false positives, rate of false negatives, and rate of classification, as well as the delivery of the data to the support vector machine's training and testing sets. Since the generated model was trained and tuned using the standard data set, it has a sufficient percentage of classification when assessing the prototype with real data in a production environment. This is because the standard data set was used for both training and tuning. When comparing different IDSs, it is helpful to compare false positive/negative rates and ROC curves of classifications. Supervised training techniques, such as SVM models, provide major advantages over rule-based processes. This is because the model is built by utilizing a statistical model that modifies its behaviour depending on the input parameters. Methods that are based on rules need participation from humans. The results show that compared to existing detection models already in use, the prototype of the proposed DDoS SVM has a high detection accuracy and reduced false positive and false negative rates.

In order to identify flooding attacks on WSN, Li et al. (2014) devised a K-Nearest Neighbor (K-NN) mechanism for detecting intrusions. As part of a wireless sensor network, the suggested K-NN algorithm is a classification algorithm. By analyzing their anomalous actions, this system can distinguish between abnormal and normal nodes. It can also analyses the intrusion detection system's choice of variables and error rate. Design and implementation of the detecting system enhanced wireless AODV routing protocol to accomplish efficient, speedy intrusion detections. The technology is capable of detecting attacks that overwhelm wireless sensor networks. Additionally, run tests to determine the impact of a flooding attack. The simulation's findings demonstrate that flooding attacks can have a significant impact on flow, particularly in bigger networks. Study the flooding attack first, then discuss the detection and preventive strategy. The experiments show how well the method halts the flooding onslaught. The test outcomes further show that the system complies with the criteria for wireless sensor network intruder detecting with high detecting efficiency and speed.

A Security Scheme Against DoS Attacks (SSAD) detection in cluster-based WSN was proposed by Han et al. (2014). Local and international trust management techniques are offered by SSAD. Nodes elect dependable cluster heads as a result of the scheme's establishment of trust management with energy characteristics. The strategy evaluates the sensor nodes in the base station's ultimate trust value as well as their present trust values in neighboring cluster heads. A novel vice cluster head node is introduced in the formal technique specifically to track a cluster head's actions. Cluster heads are protected against DoS threats using passive listening. A novel kind of vice cluster head node is also suggested in order to identify fooled cluster heads. In addition, SSAD employs an energy predictions strategy to identify fraudulent nodes that used more energy during DoS attacks. In the suggested approach, a hierarchical trust value evaluation is needed to identify malicious nodes. Theoretical investigations and simulation findings demonstrate that SSAD has a high probability of successfully preventing and identifying malicious nodes.

For the purpose of detecting anomalies and improper use in cluster-based WSN, Sun et al. (2015) created the Adaboost, Cultural-Algorithm, and Artificial-Fish-Swarm-Algorithm optimised Back Propagation (CA-AFSA-BP). An integrated detection model of cluster-based WSN, CA-AFSA-BP anomaly and misuse detection seeks to increase detection rate while lowering false rate. Cluster-based WSN with a two-level intrusion detection approach that incorporates identification of anomalies inside groups and improper usage of sink nodes. Various detection techniques are used depending on the resources that are available. For the purpose of detecting anomalies in sensor nodes, cluster-head nodes, and sink nodes, the Adaboost algorithm with hierarchical structures is utilised. The CA-AFSA-BP is used to detect Sink node misuse. Numerous simulations show that this integrated model performs well at intrusion detection.

SVM based IDSs for DoS attack detections in WSNs was proposed by Nawaz et al. in 2020. On single-class SVM-based intrusion detection. SVM can automatically construct detection models, immediately train and model the gathered data sets, and enhance the effectiveness of intrusion detection systems. Based on this technique, a three-layer intrusion detection model is developed. In data collected by cluster member nodes, the model performs better at differentiating intrusion data from routine data. Implement SVM on the QualNet simulation platform for the detection of DoS attacks and intrusion detection. The use of SVM enables the development of intruder detection systems with increased system detecting rates and decreased FARs.

For the purpose of detecting data replay attacks in WSN, Medjadba and Sahraoui (2016) created the Data Replay Intrusion Detection System (DR-IDS). Data replay attacks in WSN can be thwarted by an effective intrusion detection system. Local and broad alerts are the two different alert message kinds that make up a simple alerting system. Local alarms, which utilize minimal energy in the event that the base station was able to confirm the attacker's identity since the data was not encrypted. Depending on threshold crossing, the base station periodically increases general alerts sent. As replay attacks target the routing function, DR-IDS is designed to be integrated into the network layer, namely in the operation of routing protocols. Therefore, it must fully satisfy all of the requirements, especially those that are connected to efficiency and minimization of energy use. The proposed method is sufficiently resilient, according to the performance evaluations carried out using the NS2 simulator.

K-means Multiple Principal Component Analysis Algorithm (KMPCAA) for Application Layer Distributed Denial of Service (App-DDoS) attack detection WSN was introduced by Yang & Chang (2014).

Using an app to detect DDoS attacks KMPCAA was then proposed after it made use of Web log mining. First, a statistical characteristics feature extracting technique was developed by comparing the access patterns of legitimate users and attackers. Next, a KMPCAA was suggested utilising the maximum distance classification technique in accordance with the PCA's data dimension reduction property, and a testing model was developed using the algorithm as a foundation. Finally, utilising the CTI-DATA dataset and the simulated assault dataset, an experiment was conducted to identify App-DDoS assaults. This experiment contrasted the methods of Fuzzy Synthetical Evaluation (FSE), Hidden Semi-Markov Model (HsMM), and Dempster-Shafer Evidence Theory (D-S), as well as the suggested approach. The KMPCAA detection algorithm performs better at detection, according to experimental results.

Table 2.2 Inference of intrusion detection system

S.NO	AUTHOR NAME	METHOD NAME	ADVANTAGES	DISADVANTAGES
1	Shamshirband et al.	G-FQL	Higher detection accuracy	Not focused on various attack types detection
2	Jianjian et al.	IABRBFSVM	High identification rate for quickly identifying and deleting rogue nodes from networks during assaults	Large data collections should not be used with it
3	Ahmad et al.	LEACH and ANN	high classification rate and accuracy for detecting floods, blackhole, and grayhole assaults	Not focused on sybil/ wormhole attack detection

Table 2.2 (Continued)

4	Maleh and Ezzati	SVM	reduce communication costs, improving the lifetime of the network, high detection rate for routing attacks	Not support combination of cryptography algorithm
5	Guo et al.	AWN	high rate of detecting efficiency	Not suitable for real-time environment
6	Ma et al.	SCDNN	improves detection accuracy in real security systems	It requires very large amount of data
7	Shamshirband et al.	D-FICCA	higher detection accuracy	It is not useful for programs much smaller or larger than historical data
8	Cepheli et al.	GMMs	Once the identification is successful, reduce	The shape of the class is not flexible enough
9	Kato and Klyuev	SVMandRBF	detect DDoS assaults precisely	performs poorly when there is more noise in the data collection
10	Riecker et al.	linear regression	detected with high accuracy, false positives very low	Not suitable for larger dataset
11	Hoyos Ll et al.	SVM	high detection precision, reduced incidence of false positives and false negatives	It is not suitable for large data sets
12	Li et al.	K-NN	high detection accuracy and speed	It is only focused on flooding attack
13	Han et al.	SSAD	increased detection precision, lower incidence of false positives and false negatives	Not suitable for heterogeneous WSN

Table 2.2 (Continued)

14	Sun et al.	CA-AFSA-BP	increase detection rate and reducing false rate for mis-use detection of sink node	It may be quite susceptible to noisy data.
15	Wang et al.	SVM	more accurate system detection rates and reduced false alarms	Not suitable for real-time application in WSN
16	Medjadba and Sahraoui	DR-IDS	low energy consumption for data replay attack detection	Not focused other types of attack detection
17	Yang and Chang	KMPCAA	better detection performance	Independent variables become less interpretable

2.4 REVIEW ON OPTIMIZATION ALGORITHM IN INTRUSION DETECTION

Improved Particle Swarm Optimization (IPSO) and Back-Propagation Neural Network (BPNN), also known as IPSO-BPNN, were created by Lu et al. in 2020 for use in intrusion detection systems that can identify network threats for WSN. Provide a hierarchical structure-based intrusion detection model for WSNs. To prevent settling for the local optimum, first optimise the BPNN's initial parameters using the IPSO algorithm. Next, use IPSO-BPNN to detect intrusions using WSNs. The study's use of benchmark datasets NSL-KDD and UNSW-NB15 in simulations to evaluate the performance of the IPSO-BPNN demonstrated that IPSO-BPNN has a faster convergence speed, a greater detection accuracy rate, and a lower false positive rate when compared to BPNN and BPNN optimised by PSO algorithm, which may match the WSNs intrusion detection criterion.

The Optimized Collaborative Intrusion Detection System (OCIDS) for WSNs introduced the Improved Artificial Bee Colony (IABC) and SVM. The IABC method is used to optimize the hierarchical IDS employed by WSNs in terms of resource utilisation and intrusion detection accuracy. In addition, the suggested method enhances the weighted SVM algorithm to boost detection precision and lower FARs. Since each sensor node, cluster head, and BS in hierarchical WSNs has a unique perspective on the network, collaboration between them is taken into account to improve the projected OCIDS system's ability to identify intrusions. Effects of different assault scenarios on system efficiency are analyzed and evaluated, together with comparisons to the performance of other systems, were done to show the strength and efficiency of the suggested system. Using the NSL-KDD dataset to compare its performance to those of others under both normal and incursion traffic, it demonstrates the greatest rate of identification and the smallest percentage of false alarms. With a negligible standard deviation, the typical FARs were 1.8% of 1%, outperforming previous detection systems, and the suggested system beats them by reaching a 97.9% standard deviation is modest and the detection rate is average of 0.9%.

Particle Swarm Optimization using K-means clustering was created for the purpose of identifying routing exploits in WSN (PSO-KM). The PSO-KM-based anomaly detection approach is used in this study to find routing hazards caused by anomalous traffic. Although it is only one part of the ideal answer rather than the complete ideal solution, the K-means clustering algorithm has been successfully used to intrusion detection systems. The PSO algorithm, an evolutionary computing method based on swarm intelligence, provides efficient global search capabilities. The K-means clustering method lacks the capacity to do global searches, hence this study developed a KM clustering technique based on PSO. This algorithm had reasonably excellent overall convergence and could avoided local minimas. The suggested method's efficacy has been validated through experiments on the KDD CUP 99 data sets, which also demonstrate the method's greater detection rate and lower false detection rate.

An SVM model was developed by Kuang et al. (2015) to detect intrusions in WSNs. The model made use of KPCA and ICPSO. When determining whether or not an action constitutes an attack, the approach that is proposed uses an SVM classifier with many layers. As a preprocessor, KPCA is used to an SVM in order to lessen the dimension of feature vectors and quicken the training process. While N-RBF works to minimise noise associated with features, ICPSO works to optimise the punishment factor C, kernel parameters, and tube size of the SVM. ICPSO reduces the amount of time spent on SVM training while simultaneously improving performance via the use of chaotic optimization and premature processing. The performance of the updated SVM model outperforms the performance of the original model in terms of computation speed, prediction accuracy, and training length.For the purpose of detecting attacks in WSN, Eesa et al. (2015) developed the Cuttle Fish Optimization Algorithm (CFA) and Decision Tree (DT) in IDSs. It is a feature-selection method that is applied to IDSs and is based on the CFA. IDSs must maintain the highest quality features that accurately represent all of the data while removing any redundant or unnecessary characteristics because they deal with a lot of data. The CFA is used in the proposed model as a search method to identify the best subset of features, and the DT classifier serves as an assessment of the features that the CFA has chosen and generated. The suggested model is assessed using the KDD Cup 99 dataset. Results reveal that when compared to results obtained utilising all features, the feature subset derived using CFA delivers a greater detection rate and accuracy rate with a lower FARs.

Ali et al. (2018) designed a Fast Learning Network for intrusion detection that was based on Particle Swarm Optimization (PSO-FLN). This was done in order to identify new forms of assault in WSN. The model was validated with the use of the well-known dataset KDD99, and it was applied to the issue of intrusion detection. The effectiveness of the newly proposed model for FLN classifier and extreme learning machine training has been evaluated against a wide range of meta-heuristic techniques. The development of a particle that represents a potential FLN weight solution is the basis of FLN optimization using PSO. One particular issue with optimization is the requirement to choose the amount of neurons and weights necessary in the hidden layer to attain improved accuracy. This indicates a variable length via the solution depending on the number of FLN hidden neurons, the maximum number of neurons taken into account while determining a particle's length. In tests of the learning's accuracy, PSO-FLN has fared better than other methods.

A genetic algorithm-based eXtreme Gradient Boosting was developed by Alqahtani et al. (2019) as a method for identifying potential intrusion threats in WSN (GXGBoost). A new model based on a genetic algorithm and an extreme gradient boosting (XGBoost) classifier was provided with the purpose of identifying the potential dangers of an intrusion. The latter model makes use of gradient boosting to enhance the capability of standard models to detect attack types that are in the attack minority inside the radically uneven data flow of WSNs. The holdout and 10-fold cross validation techniques were applied in a series of experiments using the Wireless Sensor Network-Detection System (WSN-DS) dataset. The proposed approach outperforms both cutting-edge methods and other ensemble learning classifiers, according to the results of tenfold cross validation tests, which show detection accuracy rates of 99.9% or higher for regular traffic as well as flooding, scheduling, grayhole, and blackhole attacks respectively.

For the purpose of detecting DDoS attacks in WSN, Athari and Borna (2016) created the Genetic Algorithm (GA), Particle Swarm Optimization (PSO), and Glowworm Swarm Optimization (GSO). In WSN, the natural communities can serve as a paradigm. The mechanisms in these systems can be matched with a WSN. Problems with the intrusion detection system's slow convergence rate and tendency to slip into local optimality traps can be resolved with the use of PSO. Given the significant factors that influence network security, this study has looked at a model that assesses the energy and throughput of metaheuristic algorithms found in natural communities, such as PSO, GA, and GSO. The study also included active attacks with the aid of the NS2 simulator and MATLAB software since the sensor nodes in the network are crucial and because many attacks, both active and passive in nature, might endanger the security of networks. Additionally, the effect of these metaheuristic algorithms in WSN was taken into account while determining the node lifetime in WSN.

Fuzzy clustering and Improved Social Spider Optimization (ISSO) were introduced by For the identification of various assaults in WSNs, Liu et al. (2018) suggested WSN intrusion detection method based on distributed fuzzy clustering and concurrent intelligent optimization. To begin with, the framework for parallel intelligent optimization feature extraction is built on the specification of the ideal feature assessment index. The index has the potential to significantly reduce the dimensionality of the data and improve the reliability of the feature extraction process, according to the findings of the theoretical inquiry. The index may also lessen feature duplication while maintaining the diversity of the original data. Second, the inclusion of local search and a method for adaptive multi-strategy updates redefines the spider cluster optimization algorithm's evolution rule, illuminating the ISSO algorithm's global convergence. The framework for feature extraction is solved using ISSO, and the optimum feature combination is extracted using a parallel feature subset selection procedure. The performance of the fuzzy clustering algorithm is improved using three techniques: distributed fuzzy clustering technology, intelligent iterative evolution, and adaptive clustering strategy. The best feature subset is then used to perform WSN intrusion detection. The outcomes of the studies prove the intrusion detection algorithm's potency in spotting invasions. Additionally, the false detection rate is decreased by approximately 8.5%, and the intrusion detection rate is raised by about 13.1% when compared to other detection techniques.

Hajisalem & Babaie (2018) developed a hybrid classification technique based on ABC, AFS, and Fuzzy C-Means Clustering for identifying hostile infiltration or attack in WSN (FCM). Correlation-based Feature Selection removes superfluous features from the training dataset (CFS). To differentiate between regular and anomalous data, additional If-Then rules are developed using the CART approach and specified attributes. Similarly, the resultant rules teach the hybrid approach. With a 99% detection rate and a 0.01% false positive rate, simulation results on the NSL-KDD and UNSW-NB15 datasets show that the proposed approach exceeds in terms of performance metrics. The computational complexity and time costs of the proposed approach are equivalent to those of alternative approaches.

Fotohi and Bari (2020) developed the Firefly Algorithm, based on LEACH and the Hopfield Neural Network, to identify DoSA attacks in WSN (FAHN). Hopfield Neural Network, LEACH-based FA, and Mobile Sink are used in a hybrid method (FAHN). Mobile sink reduces network energy utilisation and lifespan. FA recommends clustering nodes and two-level authentication to avoid DoSA. Hopfield Neural Network determines sink movement direction and way to transfer CH data. Extensive simulations in NS-2 analyses the WSN-FAHN technique. Simulation studies comparing WSN-FAHN to contemporary schemes demonstrate that it is better in terms of performance parameters including PDRs, average throughputs, detection ratios, and network lives while reducing average residual energies.

Liu et al. (2018) enhanced Particle Swarm Optimization (IPSO) and SVM in the WSN intrusion detection model. To minimize energy use, nodes in the intrusion detection model are grouped using the modified LEACH algorithm. To provide high detection accuracy, this model leverages SVM-based anomaly detection. Finally, the SVM algorithm is optimised using the IPSO approach to get the ideal SVM parameters, which will increase the model's detection precision and convergence speed. The experimental findings demonstrate that the intrusion detection model discussed in this study provides better detection accuracy, a faster convergence time, and a more balanced use of node energy when compared to prior detection models.

Hu et al. (2015) created the Multi-hop Heterogeneous Cluster-based Optimization Algorithm to find intrusions in WSNs (MHCOA). Wireless sensor networks (WSNs) are where MHCOA takes place because, despite the fact that certain sensor nodes with higher energy consumption behave as cluster leaders and are intentionally deployed, other sensor nodes with a lower energy consumption function as cluster members and are dispersed at random. You need to complete the three major elements of this document if you want to fulfil the monitoring target. Before it can complete the monitoring operation, MHCOA must first determine the number of cluster heads and the communication range of low energy sensor nodes. Data packets are then sent through multi-hop heterogeneous WSNs using higher energy nodes that serve as cluster chiefs in the following stage of the process. In the end, it determines the longest communication distance low energy sensor nodes are capable of. According to the simulation's results, MHCOA outperforms its rivals in reducing the number of cluster heads in heterogeneous WSNs. This results in network average energy savings of up to 16.7% and network life extensions of up to 38%, while also displaying improved end-to-end latency.

MK-ELM was developed by Zhang et al. (2020) for WSN intrusion detection. WSN nodes are functionally grouped for hierarchical intrusion detection. The objective of this study is to improve the detection accuracy of aberrant WSN intrusion detection system behaviour while at the same time lowering the incidence of false alarms. To that end, it also makes use of the classification algorithm of the kernel extreme learning machine in accordance with the Mercer Property to synthesize multi-kernel functions. Build an MK-ELM for use in WSN intrusion detection systems, then make use of the multi-kernel function to determine the ideal linear combination. The method assures high detection accuracy and shortens detection time, making it perfect for WSNs with minimal resources.

Safaldin et al. (2021) introduced a modified binary Grey Wolf Optimizer with SVM-based Intrusion Detection System for WSN (GWOSVM-IDS). GWOSVM-IDS utilised 3, 5, and 7 wolves to identify optimal number. The recommended technique reduces FARs, the number of features created by WSN IDSs, and intrusion detection accuracy and rate. The NSL KDD'99 dataset is used to compare the suggested technique to others. Evaluation criteria include accuracy, amount of characteristics, execution time, FARs, and detection rate. All prior techniques were outperformed by the seven-wolf GWOSVM-IDS.

An intrusion detection system using several objectives and evolutionary algorithms was created by Thamilarasu (2015) to provide Wireless Body Area Networks with the best possible assault detection (WBAN). The management of the tradeoffs between detection accuracy, false positives, and resource consumption in WBAN is an optimization challenge. Here, genetic algorithms are specifically modeled to produce a subset of pertinent network properties required for categorizing assaults, with the goal of increasing attack detection efficiency while lowering energy consumption and false positives. Results from simulations show that the suggested detection strategy is successful, and the suggested detection system is assessed against the execution of jamming assaults. The suggested approach ensures that the intrusion detection procedure uses only the features required for identifying a specific attack, reducing the computational complexity.

Table 2.3 Inference of optimization algorithm in intrusion detection

S.NO	AUTHOR NAME	METHOD NAME	ADVANTAGES	DISADVANTAGES
1	Lu et al.	IPSO and BPNN	greater detection performance, reduced false positive rates, and quicker convergence	low iterative procedure convergence rate
2	Elsaid and Albatati	IABC and SVM	best percentage of detection and lowest number of false alarms	low efficiency and slow convergence rate
3	Li et al.	PSO-KM	greater detection efficiency and fewer false positives	For bigger datasets, it is not appropriate.
4	Kuang et al.	SVM, KPCA and ICPSO	higher predictive accuracy	low convergence rate in the iterative process
5	Eesa et al.	CFA and DT	higher detection rate and accuracy rate	They are unstable; a little change in the data may result in a significant alteration in the structure.

Table 2.3 (Continued)

6	Ali et al.	Fast Learning Network based on particle Swarm Optimization (PSO-FLN)	accuracy has increased for intrusion detection	Unexplained functioning of the network
7	Alqahtani et al.	GXGBoost	high detection rates for flooding, scheduling, grayhole, and blackhole attacks	it is very slow convergence
8	Athari and Borna	GA, PSO and GSO	high energy consumption	low accuracy computation and easy to fall into local optimum
9	Liu et al.	ISSO	improve the detection performance	Detection of tiny samples is not supported by success rate.
10	Hajisalem and Babaie	ABC, AFS and FCM	achieve high detection rate and low false positive rate	Euclidean distance measures can unequally weight underlying factors
11	Fotohi and Bari	FAHN	improve energy consumption, network lifetime and decreasing average residual energies	significant likelihood of being stuck in local optima
12	Liu et al.	IPSO and SVM	high detection accuracy and reducing energy consumption of the network	When the data collection has additional noise, it does not function very effectively.
13	Hu et al.	MHCOA	sensor nodes with greater energy serving as group heads	It is not suitable for larger datasets
14	Zhang et al.	MK-ELM	improves the detection rate	It is not focused on energy consumption
15	Safaldin et al.	GWOSVM-IDS	increase the classification precision and recognition rate for intrusions	low problem-solving efficiency, poor local search performance, and a low convergence rate

Table 2.3 (Continued)

16	Thamilarasu	genetic algorithm	decreasing the computational complexity	It is not focused on other types of attack detection

2.5 SUMMARY

In this chapter, numerous research approaches have been discussed in relation to obtaining and spotting various intrusion attacks occurring in the environment. Additionally, this part compared and analysed several research methodologies in terms of their benefits and drawbacks.

CHAPTER 3

INTRUSION AWARE DATA TRANSMISSION FRAMEWORK IN WIRELESS SENSOR NETWORK

In current scenarios and general world, studies on intrusion detections are urgently needed mainly due to hindrances in the form of attacks. This work proposes safety from intrusions in its proposal of TV-IDS (Traffic Variation based Intrusion Detection System), an enhanced version due to the usage of ANFIS for weights and GAs (Genetic Algorithms) for classifications, the hybrid genetic neuro-fuzzy classifier processes. Additionally, fuzzy based mean shift clustering is also used for clustering features. This can help to obtain accurate clustering results and has the added benefit of having a lower time complexity. The decision classifier moves this forward once the data points bias changes are assessed. This variation factor is useful in identifying the slight traffic changes and not decided to be uneven data. Specifically, a hybrid genetic Neuro fuzzy classifier is used to carry out the classification. ANFIS weights are updated concurrently with best choices using evolutionary processes. The fundamental techniques used in choosing optimum travel paths are ABC (artificial bee colony) algorithm. In order to ensure data transmissions are both efficient and practical, this technical effort takes into account a range of different fitness criteria including energy levels of nodes, bandwidths, etc.

3.1 INTRODUCTION

One function of IDSs (intrusion detection systems) is to locate attackers who attempt to access system by auditing data or network packet traffic information. Due to intrusive node collisions in networks, it increases detection costs, network activities and impeded when malicious nodes enter or exit next radio transmission ranges established at regular intervals. Compromised nodes result due to uneven physical surroundings send bogus routing information or have outdated routing tables of nodes for periods of time. The packets being lost may be due to network congestions or intruding nodes improper routing strategies.

Utilizing data from IDSs, particularly those where data analysis is involved, the security implemented (Butun et al. 2013). If traffic stream's speeds are incompatible with network's IDS requirements, the packets are dropped (Rost et al. 2015). The resources for processing may be insufficient for controlling the traffic (Nápoles et al. 2016). The high-speed links a crucial role for intruder detecting systems in network intrusion detection where there is a high demand for resources (Srbinovska et al. 2015).

The restoration of power in sensor nodes is a one more challenge considering that batteries are used for energizing the sensor nodes (Faheem et al. 2015). The reliability of the senor nodes is improved by installing them in the vicinity of the event source and sinks (Rajesh & Gnanasekar 2016). Congestion may occur in available network capacities (Ghaffari 2015) ijn increased network loads. Either increasing network capacities or decreasing network loads can be used to manage these congestions (Sergiou et al. 2014). Both the methods have their own benefits and drawbacks depending on situations. In persistent high load situations and in situations of transitory overloads, resource control mechanisms are efficient strategies and preferred for traffic control mechanisms to enhance performances (Pant et al. 2014).

In the suggested study effort, the clustering feature is implemented using a clustering feature that produces precise clustering results, illustrating the advantages of the time complexity being decreased. The decision classifier is later provided the data point bias modifications once they have been reviewed in advance. The major component that influences the minute traffic variations, which are thought to be abnormal data, is the change value. The hybrid genetic neuro fuzzy classifier, in which the ANFIS weights are updated and genetic algorithm is employed for the best selection, is introduced for classification. One other significant method used for the best route path selection is the ABC algorithm. To enhance and guarantee effective data transmission, fitness characteristics such as node energy level and bandwidth availability are calculated.

3.2 SECURED DATA TRANSMISSION FRAMEWORK

The procedure is developed by creating WSN (Wireless Sensor Networks) environment. The mean-shift clustering method based on fuzzy technology is then offered in the proposed work to carry out the clustering process, with the goal of providing accurate clustering results while reducing time complexity. In this study, the MSCA data points are first approximated before being sent to the decision classifier. In accordance with the variation value, small traffic changes will not be considered as anomalous data. Hybrid genetic neuro fuzzy classifiers have been added to GAs for modifying and choosing ANFIS weights for classification processes. Subsequently, ABC algorithm selects best routes. In order to increase data transmission rates, fitness characteristics like node energy levels and bandwidth availabilities are assessed. Figure 3.1 depicts the complete process flow of proposed technique.

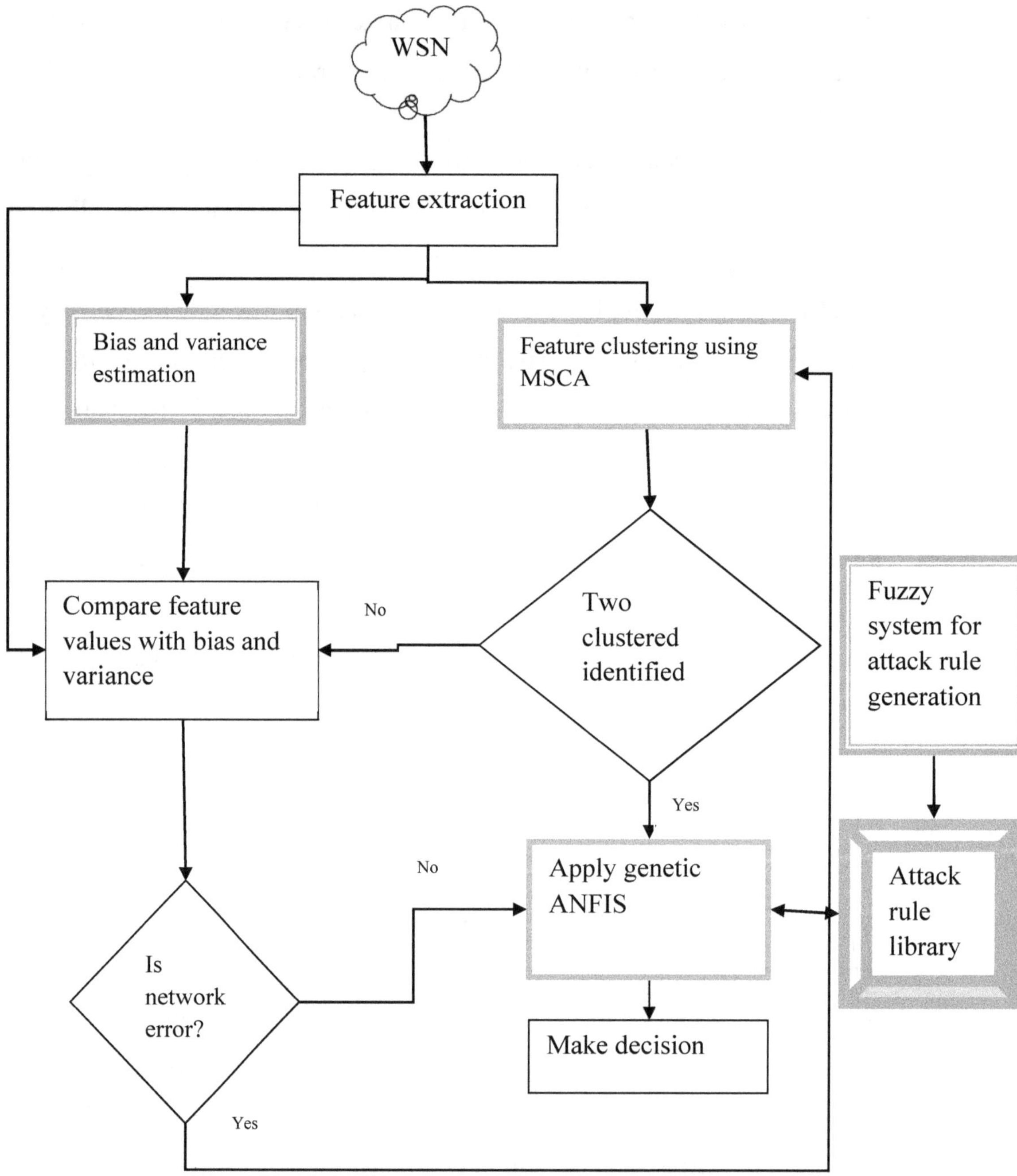

Figure 3.1 Overall processing flow of proposed work

3.3 FEATURE EXTRACTIONS

The data packet of a single intrusion assault is often permitted in protocol and content by the development of the attack system. Any internet user might potentially jeopardise the network's security, since various DDoS attack applications can be publicly accessed on the internet and anyone can download it. Intrusion attacks are found to be simple for processing, which is elaborate, degrading, sophisticated, intensive, difficult to be resisted and monitored. Therefore, in this technical work, an Intrusion feature extraction technique is suggested based on the activities of DDoS attack.

The general opinion is that traffic associated with intrusion assaults has certain intriguing characteristics when compared to "regular" traffic. Like the load measurements mentioned above, the feature extraction procedure uses a distributed probes set. However, regretfully it does notpay attention to individual features set, on the contrary uses the probes set for getting the features of different protocols layers, It also uses parameters from application layer data, such as HTTP requests (OSI Level 7), OSI Level 4 Transmission Control Protocol, and OSI Level 3 Internet Protocol packet headers. An extended data spectrum has been taken into account for the analysis, which makes it easier to categorise the traffic optimally since the chance of detecting features has increased. The collection of data from several sensors was previously helpful in attack detection, but these approaches were not included in the process for preventing intrusion. 23 features have been primarily extracted for the initial stage of this research work as given.

Table 3.1 Elementary Features

SI.No	Features	Descriptions
1	One way Ratios	The proportion of one-way connection packets to all packets
2	AverageLengthIPFlow	IP packet count split by IP traffic counts
3	RatioofInOut	the proportion of ICMP protocols to TCP and UDP protocols
4	Entropyflowlength	lengths of IP flow entropies
5	Entropyprotocols	packet entropies for the TCP, UDP, and ICMP protocols
6	Ratio TCP	TCP Ratios
7	Ratio UDP	UDP Ratios
8	RatioICMP	ICMP Ratios
9	Data Length	Data byte Packet counts delivered from sources to destinations when url flags are set
10	DSTdatalength	Counts of packets when url flags are set for counts of data bytes sent from sources to destinations
11	URG	Counts of packets where url flags are set
12	Service	port of destinations linked to services
13	Prototype	relational protocol (tcp,udp,icmp)
14	Land	connections from/to the same hosts/ports in numbers
15	Wrongfrag	Counts of wrong fragments
16	Segmenterror	Connections with SYN errors
17	Srccnt	Connections with same services
18	Dstcnt	Connections with same destination hosts
19	Syncnt	Packet counts where syn flags are set
20	Fincnt	Packet counts where fin flags are set
21	Ackcnt	Packet counts where ack flags are set
22	Pshcnt	Number of packets where psh flag is set
23	Rstcnt	Packet counts where rst flags are set

3.4 FEATURE GROUPING USING FUZZY BASEDMEAN SHIFT CLUSTERING

Since the estimated gradient has been repeatedly computed, mean shift based approaches have been identified to make it easier to approximate the comparable pixel's gradient of local density, allowing each pixel to find the same type of pixels existing inside the same picture. Even though the typical mean shift method uses radially symmetric kernels, there is a decrease in temporal coherence if the image contains noise and uneven features. To address the unfavourable behaviour of radially symmetric kernels in identifying the lower coherence, an improved mean shift approach known as anisotropic kernel mean shift has been introduced. The most efficacy is achieved using this method. The clusters of an image iterated along with the gradient of the density function until becoming static. These topics are covered in the upcoming sections of this section. The calculation of the estimated kernel density is,

$$f(x) = \frac{1}{N}\sum_{i=1}^{N} K(x - x_i) \tag{3.1}$$

With,

$$K(x) = |H|^{-0.5} K(H^{-0.5}x) \tag{3.2}$$

Where N and xi are sample counts and sample counts from an unnamed density function f, respectively. While H is an e symmetric positive definite d x dbandwidth matrix, K(•) is a compact support of a d variate kernel function that passes the regularity conditions. When referring to the Gaussian kernel, K(x) = ke(cp),, where ke(cp), signifies the convex decreasing function.

$$K_e(\varphi) = c_t e^{-\frac{\varphi}{2}} \tag{3.3}$$

And in the context of Epanechnikov kernel,

$$k_e(\varphi) = c_t \max(1 - \varphi, 0) \tag{3.4}$$

Where ct indicates the normalising constant.

When, H = h2I (I is identity matrix) used by individual global spherical bandwidths, then

$$f(x) = \frac{1}{NhctLK} \sum_{i=l} f \left(\frac{X-Xj}{h}\right) \quad (3.5)$$

Kernel densities are computed using Equation (6) as kernels are capable of separations which are radially different symmetric kernels.

$$f(x) - \sum^{N} Nb \frac{1}{hP(Hf)q} ka(d(c_i^{a}, x_j^{a}, Ha)) kP\left(\left\| \frac{(c_i - xf)}{h\beta(Hf)} \right\|^2 \right) \quad (3.6)$$

When a signifies spatial components, and refers to the temporal components, then Mahalanob is (or Euclidean) metric is expressed as $d(c^{\rho}, x_i^{q}, H_i^{a})$ as below,

$$d(c_i, x_i, H) = (x_i - c_i)^T H_i^{-1} (x_i - c_i) \quad (3.7)$$

During Anisotropic mean shifts, mean shifts aim to regulate the kernels. They try to keep the Mahalanobi distances from increasing so that basic samples may be combined. Initially, the following restrictions are used to evaluate anisotropic bandwidth matrices H i:

$$\begin{cases} k_e^{\alpha}(d(x, xi, HF)) < 1 \\ k_e\left(\left\| \frac{X - x_i}{h(Hf)} \right\|^2 \right) < 1 \end{cases} \quad (3.8)$$

The bandwidth matrix decomposition is expressed as follows

$$H_i^{\alpha} = \lambda V \, A V^T \tag{3.9}$$

Where λ represents the Scalar, whereas V and Λ indicates the normalised diagonal factors of the eigenvectors matrix and the eigen values diagonal matrix, respectively, satisfy$\prod_{i=1}^{p} a_i = 1$. Bandwidth matrices are updated by including more points in computation lists. The similarities in intensities and colours seen in these points indicate constant reductions in Mahalanobis distances, but these points are ignored in calculations when Mahalanobis distances are extended.

The recommended method combines fuzzy c-means with mean-shift segmentation. The suggested method varies greatly from prior, comparable techniques in which the states have been inherited and modified due to the shared modification of FCM and mean shift. The Mean Shift-Based FCM (MSFCM) follows the following steps:

1) Initialize the cluster nodes ci and assume that j is equal to 0.

2) Use Equation to initialise the fuzzy partitions (3.2).

3) Determine ci for each cluster using Equation (3.3) and compute j = j + 1.

4) Refresh the ij applying Equation (3.2).

5) Using Equation, provide the anisotropic kernel and matching colour radius for each pixel xi (3.17 &3.20). It should be observed that the FCM output picture has mean shift accentuated.

6) Once the mean shift M+(xi)M(xi) is lower than a pixel, evaluate the vector of mean shift by comparing the variance between the starting location and a normalised position (v = 0.5).

$$M+(xJ$$
$$= vM\text{-}(xi)$$
$$+\ (1-v)\frac{\sum_{j=1}^{N}(x_j - M^-(x_i))\left\|(M^-(x_i^{\beta}) - x_j^{\beta})/(h^{\beta}H_j^{\alpha})\right\|^2}{\sum_{j=1}^{N}\left\|(M-(x_i^{\beta}) - x_j^{\beta})/(h^{\beta}H_j^{\alpha})\right\|^2}$$

(3.10)

7) Combine the similarcolour pixels.

8) Re-execute Steps 3 to 6 till convergence is attained.

3.5 DECISION MAKING USING GENETIC NEURO CLASSIFIER

When learning about clustering attacks, it helps to understand the nodes' packet-forwarding capabilities. The self-adaptive routing protocols get better since the knowledge obtained via learning is primarily used in the routing process right away. The implementation of learning node behaviour finds extensive use of the hybrid genetic fuzzy neural network method. In this case, the GFNN (Genetic Fuzzy Neural Network) method is comparable to the Suzuki Controller. In the m unique property dimensions, the membership functions vector $\hat{f} = (\mu_1, \ldots, \mu_m), \check{f}: x \rightarrow [0, e]$ execute fuzzifications of crisp input vectors xp$\in$ $R^{m \times 1}$, where e represents dimensional unit vector. T-norm collects fuzzy vectors $\hat{f}$ to fuzzy signals, i.e. ap =T (f(xp)) while X specifies input features xj, associated with memberships linguistic property single sets, i.e. poor, medium, and good. Also, 3m fuzzifiers specify m-dimensional patterns x=(xl,...,xm), instead of abovementioned fuzzy vectors with unique properties.

$$\mathbf{f} = (\mu 1,\text{poor}, \mu 1,\text{medium}, \mu 1,\text{good}, \cdots, \mu m,\text{gooct}) \tag{3.11}$$

The π -function may now be applied to express the membership in a proper manner. The approach heavily relies on the aggregated signal defuzzification. Each fuzzy output cluster's signal mapping is carried out using a vector h=(μG1,.....,μGk), so a suitable T-conorm aggregates it into crisp group indicator, S(a,b) :=1 - T(1 - , a1 - b), a,bE[0, 1]. Each crisp input, each set of fuzzy outputs, and the requirement for various membership functions are taken into account. In order to calculate the final group membership for an observation xp, the following function is used.

$$g_p \quad ig \; (S(h(ap)))$$

$$= ig \; (S(h(T(f(Xp))))) \tag{3.12}$$

When necessary, $\tilde{f}$ is suitably collected across the linguistic characteristics for each characteristics in x, which is to state that,

$$\mathbb{R}^{m\times 1} 3\, \mathbf{f}$$

$$= (S(\mu 1,\text{poor}, \mu 1,\text{medium}, \mu 1,\text{gooct}), \cdots, S(\mu m,\text{poor}, \mu m,\text{medium}, \mu m,\text{gooct})) \tag{3.13}$$

The degree of the argument of the iarg(.)-function, which is connected to the observation of pth, is group membership in Gi. Thus, iarg(.) yields the group index that the S-norm identified. When each feature is given a unique set of linguistic traits, the first hidden layer is split into two sections: one shows the collection of properties, while the other displays them for each feature individually.

For the corresponding inputs xj; j=1,...,m throughout this work, the degree of membership that the fuzzifierf (first hidden layers) of fuzzy sets indicate excellent economic indicators or low/medium/ good economic indicators appropriately, if necessary. The mapping functionh repeatedly expresses the membership degree in each group of the fuzzy outputs, as initiated by aggregated signald α_p

THE GFNN-ALGORITHM

The primary Hybrid GFNN's steps are described in the section after, and group membership in Gi is used as the argument of the iarg(.)-function, which is tied to the observation ofpth. As a result, iarg(.) produces the group index that the S-norm found. The first hidden layer is divided into two portions when each feature is given a distinct set of linguistic traits: one displays the qualities collectively, while the other does so for each feature separately.

The degree of membership that the fuzzifierf (first hidden layer) of the fuzzy set indicates for the associated inputs xj; j=1,...,m throughout this study comprises the superior economic indicators (or otherwise, low, medium, and good economic indicators appropriately, if necessary). A quick description of the mapping functionh, which continually conveys the membership degree in each group of the GFNN algorithm Assume that L and LMAX represent the predetermined number of operations, and that T represents the most iterations that may be performed during stages 1-4.

Step 0: To the fuzzifier (f) and the defuzzifier (h), specify the membership functions. Define the modification metrics ($\tilde{f}$and $\tilde{h}$ learning rates). Actuate the bounds for $w=(\tilde{f}^T, \tilde{h}^T)^T$ to the given values [left, right]. Consider t=0, specifyF(w, t) and the population is activated

$$\text{POP}(t) = \begin{bmatrix} w_{1t} \\ \vdots \\ . \\ w_{Nt} \end{bmatrix} = \begin{bmatrix} (x_{1t}, y_{1t}) \\ \vdots \\ . \\ (x_{Nt}, y_{Nt}) \end{bmatrix} \tag{3.14}$$

Where, w_{It} indicates the actual (current optimal) solution, wit ∈[left, right], ∀i.

Step 1: Utilizing F(w; ρt+(L−1)T) in the form of trails, evaluate and rank POP(t) in ascending order. Include the observation and assign a category. If$\hat{g}_p$=gp, go to step 2, otherwise move on to step 3.

Step 2: Assign the membership functions for the sets of false and true fuzzy output to and $_{gp}$. Use the $_{gp}$ learning ratio to infinitesimally change the convexity/concavity of the functions, making the true group more dependable and the false set less reliable.

Go to step 3 if$\hat{g}_p$ =gp; otherwise, alter the convexity/concavity of the essential membership function(s) in the fuzzifierf infinitesimally, that is, the function(s) that activate the vector mapping function h from the aggregate signal. Therefore, the true set has more dependability while the false set has lower reliability depending on the fiing level of the changed signal.

3rd Step: Choose the N=2 best individuals from POP(t), then create N new persons in POP(t + 1) using arithmetic mixed-integer crossover and non-uniform mixed-integer mutation.

To achieve convergence, repeat steps 1 through 3; otherwise, move up to L=LMAX. The stop condition is as follows: After a certain number of repetitions, the ideal values of the objective function are expected to have a moving average that is and If $|Ft-\bar{F}_t| < \varepsilon$ is true, then stop executions.

3.6 OPTIMAL ROUTE PATH SELECTION

The ABC Algorithm was created on the basis of the cunning behaviour of bees. It is a typical optimization technique that Karaboga published in 2005 for distributed search goals. With the aid of their nest mates, the bees are able to locate the food source and change their locations accordingly. If the artificial bees are inexperienced, they pick the food source themselves. When a bee forgets the location of a prior food supply, it is nevertheless capable of remembering the position of a superior new nectar source. The exploration and exploitation operations of ABC are balanced by observers and worker bees by conducting a local search with them in addition to the global search with drones.

While the scout bee conducts exploration in ABC, the hired bees and observer bees are in charge of exploitation in the search zone. The employment rate and intake of new food sources at the swarm's location are assessed. The ability of the bees to live gives them the capacity to swiftly find the best solutions. The number of bees participating in ABC is almost equal to the main food source. In order to model and develop the forward path progress as well as to resolve optimum routing issues, ABC is used. The neighbour node nectar, which is regarded as food, is the parameter employed in this study to assess the bandwidth at the forward point. When the messages are in different states and the common method needs to be rebuilt, the table-driven algorithm is mostly used.

A very large network model that might become a constraint in the future may find that the geographic information is a constraint. The foundation for message transfer is established by the router intelligence and data acquired environmental variables, such as the amount of bandwidth available at a high forward node's angular alignment of the forward vector, and QoS elements like jitter and delay, etc. The exploitation is carried out by hired bees who are given random assignments. Fitness is a key factor for the employed bee when deciding on the local food source and nectar evaluation during the complete iteration. Ni represents the location of the ith food supply Ni ϵ(n1, n2, ...ne). In this case, denotes the potential connectable nodes. The entire amount of nectar that Ni will probably be able to offer is given by the expression F(ni). With the probability pi computed as follows, the observer bee finds the location of the food source at Ni:

$$p_i = \frac{F(N_i)}{\sum_{k=1}^{f} F(n_k)} \tag{3.15}$$

where fs is the total number of available food sources. The amount of nectar at node Ni is used as the numerator, while the total amount of nectar collected from the present node and all of its neighbours is used as the denominator. The dance now determines how much useable free bandwidth is available. The quantity of bees flying toward the node is determined by the bandwidth available. The outcome of intermediary pathways is presented as Fmax1, derived from the filtered greatest value across all of the current node's neighbours and becomes the current node's first neighbour. The = symbol here defines the update on the intermediary paths of the current node. By extending the following equation, where the + symbol indicates the development of an intermediate link from the current node to the node with the largest available bandwidth in the direction of the target, the observer finds Ni's local food source and feeds it.

$$N_i(n_i + 1) = C_i(n_i) + F^{w}_{max1}(C_i(n_i)) \tag{3.16}$$

The group of watchful bees assists in selecting the following intermediate node. Finding the number of spectator bees requires knowing how many neighbours each node, represented by w, possesses. The current intermediate node is indicated by $C_i(n_i)$, while the neighbour from the current intermediate node choice is designated as $F^{w}_{max1}(C_i(n_i))$. Fmax1 w, the neighbour of the current intermediate node with the largest bandwidth, retrieves the node address from the database. The outcome is determined by concatenating the current node with the subsequent intermediate route. $C_i(n_i)$ has been modified thus far as,

$$C_i(n_i) = N_i(n_i + 1) \tag{3.17}$$

The procedure is continued until the desired result is obtained; otherwise, no more links are established for research.

The router that will enable speedy message transmission is chosen with the help of the threshold bandwidth. Finding the nodes that meet the network awareness requirements for the QoS measure simplifies the routing choice. The fitness value is calculated when the neighbours have been determined. The bees go to a different food source each time the new fitness value rises over the old value or pauses at the same node. The information is distributed to interested bees once all hired bees have finished searching for food sources. As a result, pi determines the chance that these food sources will be picked, as indicated by (1), which represents the optimal bandwidth on the link between Ni (t) and Ni (t+1) using vigilant bees. The following describes the ABC pseudocode used for network routing:

Initialize the bandwidth and nodes at random.

The hired bees are mostly used as a source of neighbours.

REPEAT

When the hired bees are moving along their tracks, the fitness is calculated.

The report on the data gathered is given to the spectator bees by the hired bees.

The number of spectator bees to move depends on the maximum bandwidth.

Scout bees (different quadrant search is triggered) are used in the search process if a good node (meaning no link with appropriate bandwidth) is not found.

Remember best nodes obtained.

UNTIL (stop conditions are met)

3.6.1 Fitness Evaluation

The total energy E_t consumed

$$E_t(s_i, d) = \begin{cases} s_i E + s_i \varepsilon_{fs} d^2, d \leq d_0 \\ s_i E + s_i \varepsilon_{mp} d^2, d > d_0 \end{cases} \tag{3.18}$$

$$d_o = \sqrt{\frac{\varepsilon_{fs}}{\varepsilon_{mp}}} \tag{3.19}$$

Where, E indicates the energy depleted for the sending or receiving of 1 bit message; ε_{fs} is used to indicate the free-space signal's amplifying efficiencyand ε_{mp}stands for the signal enhancement factor for multi-path fade, their values are determined by the circuit amplifier model; d indicates the separation between the transmitter and receiver; and s i indicates the bit rate of transferring information.

Since nodes present between a node's transmission and interference range will consume the bandwidth of each node, the data is transferred according to the estimated bandwidth. As far as data transmission is concerned, the node requires the confined bandwidth and knowledge about its nearby mobile nodes that are in interference range. The node may determine the channel and the local bandwidth by using the bandwidth shared by nearby nodes (BW_L) is evaluated. It purely depends on an inactive and active period ratio for a preset duration.

$$BW_L = C_{CH} * (T_i/T_{in}) \tag{3.20}$$

Where C_{CH} notates the channel capacity, T_i indicates the idle period and T_{in} indicates the predetermined period. The earlierset of neighboring node information is useful in deciding the minimum bandwidth (**BWmin**) of all the nodes present within the interference range. Therefore, the difference among **BWmin** and BW_L yields the BW of thenode.

$$Bw = BW_L - BW_{min} \tag{3.21}$$

3.7 RESULTS AND DISCUSSION

Through the MATLAB environment, the empirical results of the effectiveness of the suggested ways have been evaluated. The BS was positioned in the centre of the network system using the network topology of heterogeneous nodes with a dimension of 100m x 100m, which are randomly spread with starting energies varying between 0.5J and 2.25J. For each procedure, the system's average energy consumption, which totals 102.5J, has been assured to be identical. Additionally, these regimens' individual efficacy has been developed by using their best parameters.

Through metrics like Detection Rates, FARs, Precisions, and Recalls, the effectiveness of the recommended solutions has been evaluated. Through simulation, the ensuing performance measures have been obtained to establish. The PCACID and KBIDS existing techniques have now been contrasted with the recommended TV-IDS methodology. The performance of the techniques is determined by a variety of measurements, but it essentially depends on four characteristics, i.e. TP: True Positive True is acknowledged True, True Negative (TN), False is acknowledged as being incorrect False Positive (FP): True is classified as False (appropriate identification). False Negative (FN): False is identified as false (incorrect identification). True (incorrect identification) (incorrect identification).

Detection Rate

The rate cost for detecting antigens by the sensor nodes is understood to be the detection rate.

$$\text{Detection Rate} = \frac{\text{TP}}{\text{TP} + \text{FN}} \tag{3.22}$$

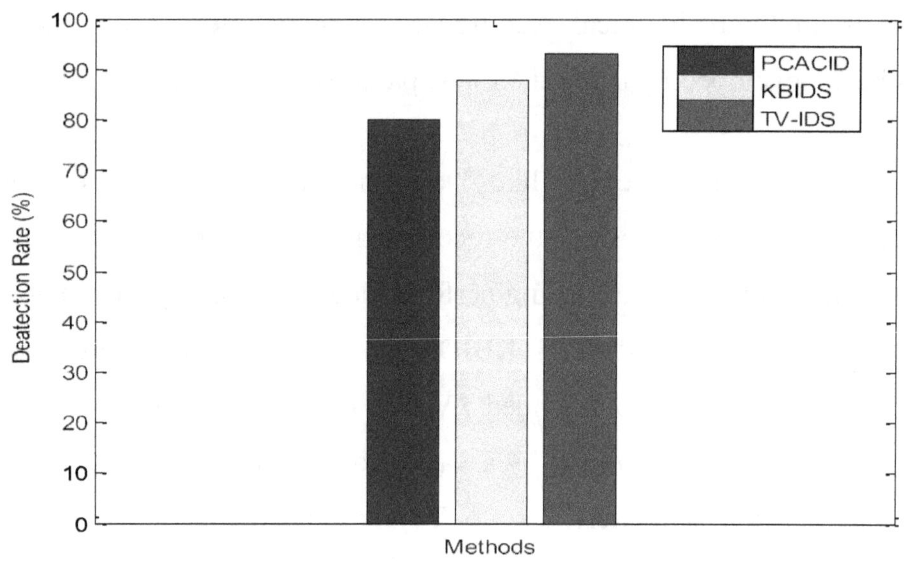

Figure 3.2 Detection rate comparison graph

The detection rate comparison chart, which is shown in Figure 3.2, displays the number of attacking nodes, network data traffic, and unidentified antigens that have been processed by nodes. As a result, the detection rates of all three algorithms are rising. Compared to alternative approaches like PCACID and KBIDS, the recommended TV-IDS technique appears to have a very high detection rate because it costs so much to identify nodes using this algorithm.

FARs (False Alarm rates)

In FARs, FP stands for false positive and TN for true negative, represents the false positive ratio as well as the total self-samples identified by the detector set.

$$\mathrm{FAR} = \frac{\mathrm{FP}}{\mathrm{FP} + \mathrm{TN}} \tag{3.23}$$

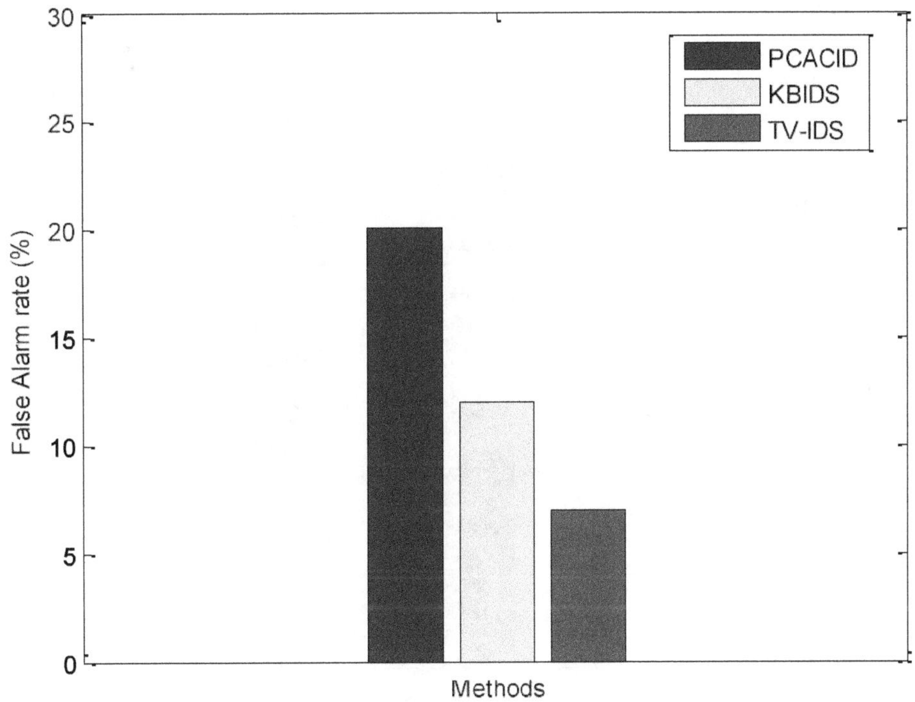

Figure 3.3 Comparative Graphs of FARs

The results of FARs are contrasted in Figure 3.3. The graph shows that the suggested TV-IDS technique gains a lower FARs than the KBIDS and PCACID algorithms that are already in use.

Precisions

Precisions are often referred to as system accuracies. The following phrase can be used to calculate the ratio of real positives to expected positives.

$$\text{Precision} = \frac{\text{TP}}{\text{TP} + \text{FP}} \times 100 \tag{3.24}$$

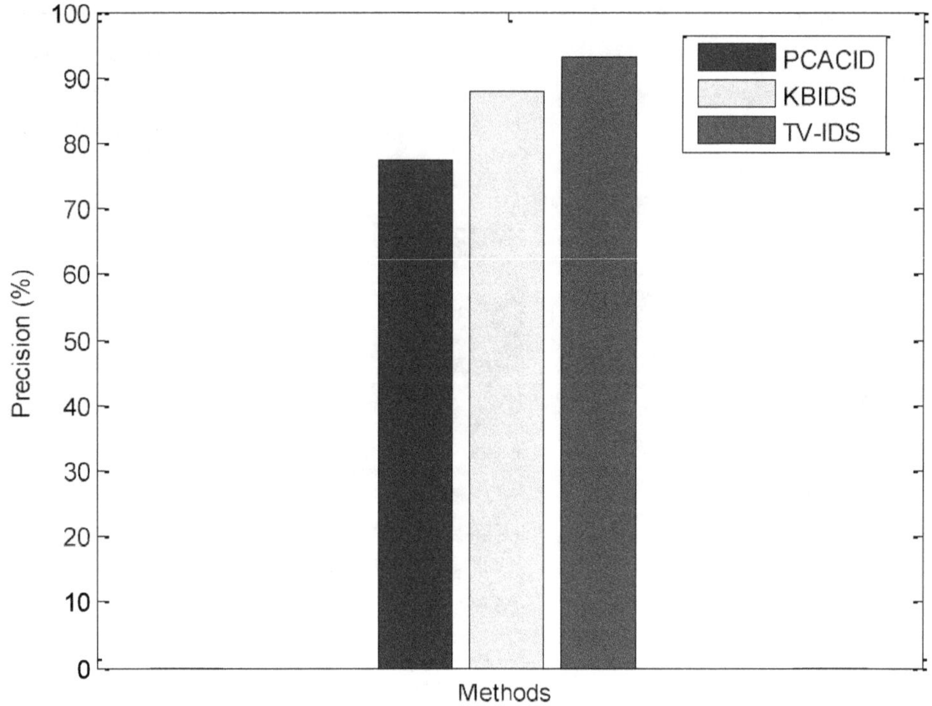

Figure 3.4 Precision comparison graph

The precision findings are analysed and compared in Figure 3.4, where it is shown that the recommended TV-IDS technique has a higher precision value than the KBIDS and PCACID algorithms currently in use.

Recalls

Recall rates are computed as:

$$\text{Recall/Sensitivity} = \frac{\text{TP}}{\text{TP} + \text{FN}} \times 100 \tag{3.25}$$

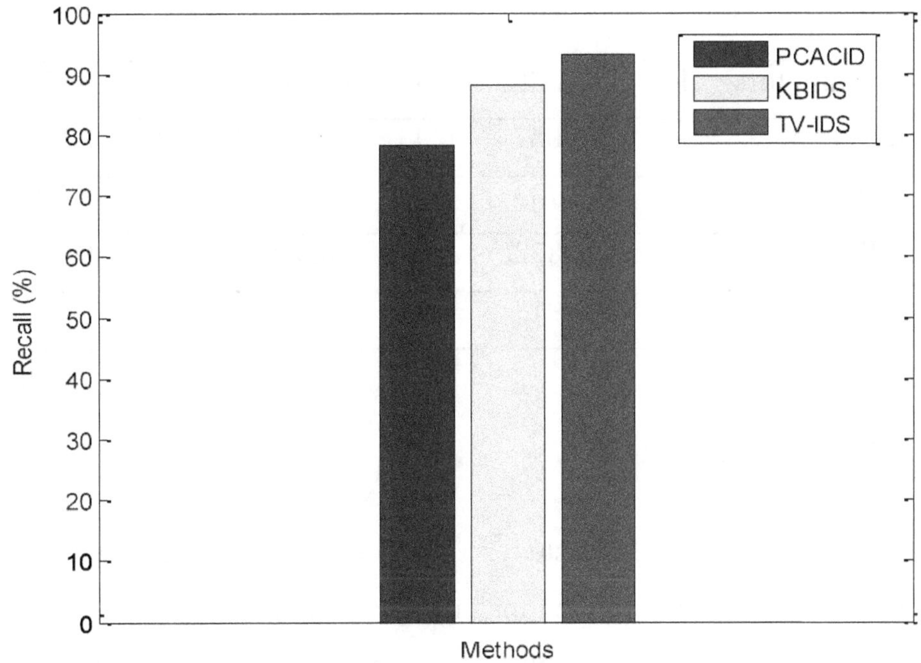

Figure 3.5 Recall comparison graph

Figure 3.5 shows a chart that compared the Recall by looking at the results. In which it is said that the KBIDS and PCACID current algorithms fall short of the optimal recall rate when compared to the advised TV-IDS technique.

The recommended techniques are thoroughly contrasted in Table 3.2 with regard to the crucial factors taken into account throughout the assessment process.

Table 3.2 Overall comparison of the parameters

Parameters	PCACID	KBIDS	TV-IDS
Detection Rates	79.9087	88	93
Precisions	77.3733	87.9752	92.9937
Recalls	78.0822	88.0208	92.9937
FARs	20.0913	12	7

3.8 SUMMARY

In the suggested study, a mean-shift clustering based on a fuzzy technique has been established for the process of clustering features, with the goal of producing a flawless clustering output with a minimal amount of time complexity. In this work, the bias variation of the data points has been estimated before being fed into the decision classifier. Minor traffic variations won't result in anomalous data based on the value of variance. The classification procedure in this study uses a hybrid genetic neuro-fuzzy classifier, and the genetic algorithm also aids in optimising the revision and selection of the ANFIS weights. The ABC algorithm eventually selected the best route to take. The current fitness factors for enhancing the success rate of data transfer are the node energy level and the availability of bandwidth. The complete evaluation of this research was conducted using the MATLAB simulation environment, since the recommended TV-IDS was designed to provide the highest level of efficiency.

CHAPTER 4

SECONDARY SERVER-BASED COMPUTATION OVERHEAD REDUCED FRAGMENTATION ATTACK DETECTION IN WIRELESS SENSOR NETWORK

The idea of fragmentation attack detection is the aspect of this research, which provides an overview of secondary Server integration. This technique would place a secondary server between the receiver and transmitter nodes, through which data packets would be sent. Here secondary server selection is done by using the method Improved genetic algorithm. As discussed in the previous work Bias and Variance estimation is done to improvise the overall processing of the research work. Finally, Truncated SVM algorithm is introduced to learn and predict the presence of an attack. Optimal route path selection is done using Modified Mosquito Swarm Algorithm to select the shorter route path to transmit the data packet with reduced delay. Attack prevention is ensured by introducing the Modified Double key encryption procedure to be encrypted before transmission.

4.1 INTRODUCTION

It may be challenging to utilise the widely accepted network environments which are interactions and multi-hop wireless communications between sink nodes and multiple sensors in different applications of WSNs (1Tomić. I & McCann 2017). This is the case for hostile circumstances where gathering sensory data and managing the network in real-time may be challenging, such as battlefields and unreachable places.

Hamami & Nassereddine (2019). in these specific cases, itinerant sinks are employed to collect sensing data per demand (Soni & Shrivastava 2018). Shortly, we may imagine brand-new Internet of Things (IoT) services made out of high-tech gadgets, such autonomous unmanned aerial vehicles (UAVs), that would serve as sink nodes in a sensor network and provide these features (Tanyingyong et al. 2021). Unattended Wireless Sensor Networks is the name given by researchers to this kind of sensor network design. (UWSN) (Kapusta et al. 2019).

Data survival, which analyses whether data produced by a sensor node is efficiently transported to an itinerant sink node, is one of the more important aspects of UWSN (Lim et al. 2020). This is crucial in UWSN since unattended sensors must store data until an itinerant sink gets near enough to receive it (Choi et al. 2018). During this time, attackers who are also mobile may be able to steal, change, or destroy data from sensor nodes (Mrugala et al. 2017)

Data fragmentation (Brinck et al. 2017) is one of the proposed solutions for improving data survival. The goal of data fragmentations are to split data sets k into fk fragments using cryptographic methods. An itinerant sink collecting can decode the data f'_k number of fragments where $f'_k \leq fk$. If the f'_k is high enough, an attacker will have to attack many sensors to collect, f'_kFragments make it more difficult for them to exploit the data properly. Therefore, data fragmentation protects offering adaptability even if part of the pieces is lost or are not retrieved by the nomadic sink node, while also protecting the data themselves (Kakatkar & Spann 2019).

The bulk of the state-of-the-art in data fragmentation, however, solely takes security into account when deciding how to split and defragment the data (Alsirhani et al. 2017). Despite the fact that there may be many deployed sensors in a sensor network, they do not take this into account when deciding where to put the pieces, the circumstances under which sensors may receive a data fragment, however, can be somewhat variable. Furthermore, multi-hop routing techniques are required in order to send data to distant sensors. Since multi-hop routing is not required by the UWSN architecture as a whole, adding a routing layer simply to convey data fragments results in significant energy and bandwidth usage from control packet transmission (Manasa). Although several strategies for epidemic flooding have been presented to distribute data to far sensor nodes, these approaches only reproduce the same data with different features and goals from data fragmentation (Stylidou et al. 2020). Because fragmented data varies in detail, it is challenging to employ epidemic methods to propagate data pieces without incurring significant overhead.

In this research work, the fragmentation attack detection concept is focused. The computation overhead is significantly lowered by adapting the secondary server concept, which will carry out the data transmission process. Changes in data transmission are detected by utilizing the bias and variance concept as in previous research work. Based on these variances, attack detection is detected by utilizing the truncated SVM algorithm. Finally, optimal route path selection is made to improvise efficient data transmission. Security of the data transmission is guaranteed by utilizing the modified Double key encryption.

4.2 SECONDARY SERVER-BASEDFRAGMENTATION ATTACK DETECTION

The idea of fragmentation attack detection is the aspect of this research, which provides an overview of secondary Server integration.

This technique would place a secondary server between the receiver and transmitter nodes, through which data packets would be sent.

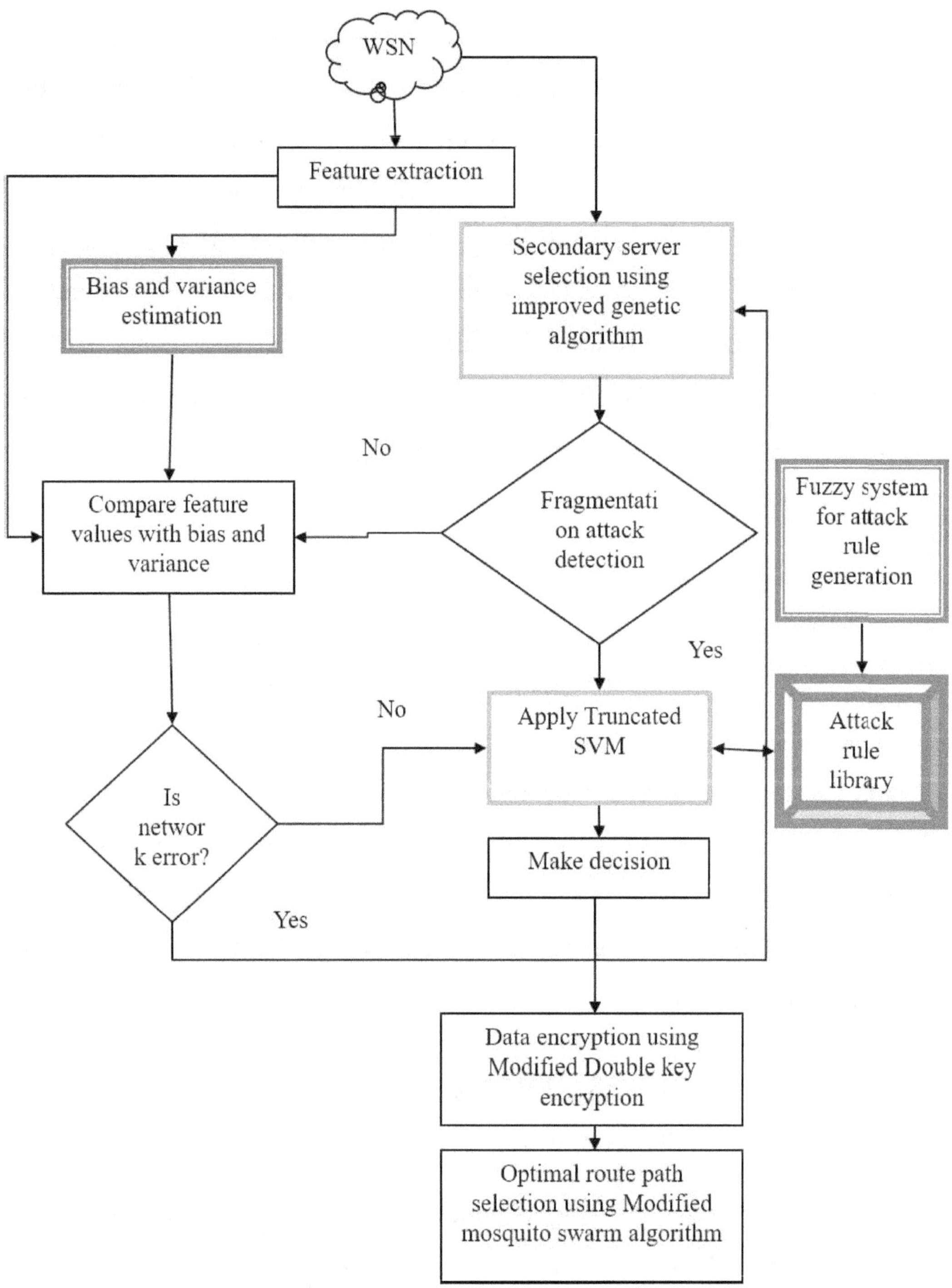

Figure 4.1 The processing flow of the suggested approach

Adaptive genetic algorithms were used to select backup servers while Bias and Variance estimations executed based on previous proposals improvised overall processes. Finally, Truncated SVM algorithm is introduced to learn and predict the presence of an attack. Optimal route path selection is done using Modified Mosquito Swarm Algorithm to select the shorter route path to transmit the data packet with reduced delay. Attack prevention is ensured by introducing the Modified Double key encryption procedure to be encrypted before transmission. Figure 4.1 illustrates the processing sequence.

4.3 SECONDARY SERVER SELECTION USING IMPROVED GENETIC ALGORITHM

In the second research method, fragmentation attack detection is concentrated on improving network performance by introducing the secondary Server integration concept. This method would install the secondary server between the receiver and the sender nodes through which data packets would be transmitted. This secondary server selection is carried out to ensure the chosen secondary server is secured and trustworthy to verify the attacker's presence. This is done by introducing the clustering concept where the set of distributed sensor nodes are clustered together, cluster head selection is done. Here, a better genetic method is used to choose the heads of the clusters, which can select the most optimal cluster head to choose the available secondary server that can fulfill the requirement. This secondary server would check for fragmentation attacks by using the IP header details to ensure successful detection of attacks. The overall attack detection performance is improved by integrating this fragmentation detection concept to ensure data transmission.

Here the secondary server is selected using an improved genetic algorithm. By merging the crossover with the mutation process, the enhanced genetic algorithm modifies the crossover. By measuring the variation of genes, a diversity-based mutation strategy selects the gene to be crossed across. Heuristic searches based on Charles Darwin's idea of natural evolutions are known as genetic algorithms. When the best individuals are picked, natural selection begins. They produce offspring who inherit their parents' characteristics and contribute to the following generation. Children with physically active parents will be healthier and have longer survival times. The best people are discovered after repeating this procedure.

Crossover points are chosen at random in traditional genetic algorithms, which may reduce accuracy. The accuracy is enhanced by developing an improved genetic algorithm. Rather than selecting crossover points at random, diversity-based mutation is used to choose best crossover points.

In this mutation scheme, a variable with less population-wise diversity is assigned a higher mutation chance. To do so, first, compute the variance of each variable's values overall population members, then arrange the variables in ascending order of variance. After that, i [0, $\in$ n − 1] an exponential probability distribution ($p(i) = \lambda \exp(-\lambda i)$) for $i \in [0, n-1]$ is utilized.

4.3.1 Improved Genetic Algorithm

The secondary server is selected using an Improved Genetic Algorithm dependent on the availability of resources and trust. After the secondary server has been selected, data is forwarded to the sink node using the least transmission power available. A node with the highest trust, energy, and resource availability has a higher chance of becoming a server. Suppose two of the parameters have maximum values while the other has a low value. In that case, the chance of that node becoming a secondary server is determined by the weights assigned to that parameter.

Algorithm for selecting Cluster Heads using Secondary Servers

1. Make a starting population of chromosome-containing people that aren't all the same.

2. Assess each person's fitness and place them in ranking order.

3. Individuals with the best fitness function for reproduction should be selected.

4. Delete some fewer solutions from the set.

5. Reintegrate the optimal individuals.

    Consider two individuals, c1 and c2

    Employ diversity based mutation of c1

        Return gene g1 (node) with more variance

    Employ cross over between c1 and c2 on position g1

6. Analyze the fitness levels of the changed people.

7. Create a new population.

4.4 BIAS AND VARIANCE ESTIMATION

As mentioned in the previous study, Bias and Variance estimate improves the research work's security. We assume that all WSN sensors can have some error; such error e_s^t of a sensor, s is characterized by the Gaussian distribution random variable with a sensor bias bs and sensor variance σ_s e_s^t ~ N(bs, σ_s^2). Let rt denote the signal's value at time t. Each sensor readi x_s^t can be represented as follows:

$$x_s^t = r_t + e_s^t \tag{4.1}$$

As true value rt cannot be used, e_s^t cannot be acquired. However, the values of the differences of errors can be acquired. Thus,if $\delta(i, j) = \frac{1}{m}\sum_{t=1}^{m}(x_i^t - x_j^t)$, then

$$\delta(i,j) = \frac{1}{m}\sum_{t=1}^{m}(x_i^t - x_j^t) = \frac{1}{m}\sum_{t=1}^{m} e_i^t - \frac{1}{m}\sum_{t=1}^{m} e_j^t \tag{4.2}$$

in which e_i^t denotes random variable with Gaussian distribution e_i^t~ N (bs, σ_s^2). Let $\bar{e}_i = \frac{1}{m}\sum_{t=1}^{m} e_i^t$ is the sample mean of this random variable.

$$\delta(i,j) = \bar{e}_i - \bar{e}_j \approx b_i - b_j \tag{4.3}$$

Here bias vector b = [bl, b2,... ,bn] and sensor readings { x }, matrices $\{\hat{x}_s^t\}$ and { (i,j)} are described as below:

$$\hat{x}_s = x_s^t - b_s \tag{4.4}$$

$$\beta(i,j) = \frac{1}{m-1}\sum_{t=1}^{m}\left((x_i^t - x_j^t) - (b_i - b_j)\right)^2 \tag{4.5}$$

By (1), we have $x_i^t - x_j^t = (r_t + e_i^t) - (r_t + e_j^t) = e_i^t - e_j^t$; thus, we obtain

$$(i,j)= \frac{1}{m-1}\sum_{t=1}^{m}(e_i^t - b_i)^2 + \frac{1}{m-1}\sum_{t=1}^{m}(e_j^t - b_j)^2 - \frac{2}{m-1}\sum_{t=1}^{m}(e_i^t - b_i)(e_j^t - b_j) \tag{4.6}$$

Consider that independent random variables produce the sensors noise; The sampling mean is approximated using the bias bi variate; as a result

$$\frac{1}{m-1}\sum_{t=1}^{m}(e_i^t - b_i)(e_j^t - b_j) \approx Cov(e_i, e_j) = 0 \tag{4.7}$$

and also

$$\beta(i,j)= \frac{1}{m-1}\sum_{t=1}^{m}(e_i^t - b_i)^2 + \frac{1}{m-1}\sum_{t=1}^{m}(e_j^t - b_j)^2 = \sigma_i^2 + \sigma_j^2 \tag{4.8}$$

The variance of sensors' noise is validated by calculating the matrix -

4.5 TRUNCATED SVM FOR ATTACK LEARNING AND DETECTION

To identify the presence of an attack, the Truncated SVM algorithm is introduced, and redesigned the pinball loss and applied the new loss function to the SVM model. We make the negative half of the pinball loss flat at a preset location -s as the horizontal part of the loss function curve is related to the sparsity, and -s is the hinge point. Simultaneously, because all correctly categorized points are penalized, this adjustment maintains the loss of pinball feature sensitivity to noise. We call it "the truncated pinball loss" because of the curvature of the function curve.

An auxiliary function is employed: **H.(u)** = max{Tu, 0}{Vu E **R}**In which T is a constant. Also, truncated pinball loss is described as:

$$P_{\tau,s}(u) = H_{1+\tau}(u) - (H_{\tau}(u + s) - \tau s) \tag{4.9}$$

$$\begin{cases} \tau s & (u \le -s) \\ -\tau u & (-s < u < 0) \\ u & (u \ge 0) \end{cases}$$

Where $0 \leq \tau \leq 1$.

Algorithm:

Input: $L^0 := 0$, $U^0 := (1 + \tau)Ce$, $\alpha^0 := 0$, $\varepsilon > 0$, $k == 0$

Output: The solution α^* and the decision function

Repeat

Project α^k $L^k \leq \alpha \leq U^k$ And set the result as the initial value

Solve the following problem

$$\min_{\alpha} \frac{1}{2} \alpha^T Q \alpha - e^T \alpha$$

$$\text{s.t. } \alpha^T Y e = 0, L \leq \alpha \leq U$$

Set the solution as α^{k+1}

Calculate b^{k+1}

Compute δ^{k+1}

$$L^{k+1} := -\delta^{k}$$

$$U^{k+1} := (1+\tau)Ce - \delta^{k+1}$$

Calculate function value of $\hat{J}(\alpha^{k+1})$

K:=k+1

Until k>1 and $\left|\left(\hat{J}(\alpha^{k}) - \hat{J}(\alpha^{k-1})\right)/\hat{J}(\alpha^{1})\right| < \epsilon$

4.6 OPTIMAL ROUTE PATH SELECTION USING MODIFIED MOSQUITO SWARM ALGORITHM

The Modified Mosquito Swarm Algorithm is used to locate the most direct way with the least amount of delay to transmit the data packet. The route path is chosen based on the calculation of the above criteria for each node in the WSN. The Modified Mosquito Swarm Technique (MMSA) algorithm chooses the routing path nodes in a wireless sensor network. The MMSA algorithm considers node position, residual energy, and available bandwidth when determining each node's route path and weight throughout the network. The fitness assessment, in this case, is calculated using the Pareto optimality methodology. As a result, the MMSA can produce more accurate predictions than the typical mosquito swarm method.

Design the Mosquito Swarm Algorithm (MSA), Mosquitoes (gnats) have senses that allow them to track their prey: A) Mosquitoes have chemical sensors that allow them to smell lactic acid and carbon dioxide up to 36 meters away. These gases are produced by the regular breathing of mammals and birds. Some substances in sweat seem to also attract insects. B) Heat sensors, Mosquitoes can detect heat, allowing them to locate warm-blooded creatures and birds quickly. A mosquito swarm can be seen in areas where there is standing water.

For most multi-objective optimization issues, performance enhancement of one target will decrease the accuracy of the other. To achieve a balanced optimization, the Pareto optimal solution notion is employed in this study. The Pareto concept can deal with the paradoxical relationship between numerous optimization objectives. It is frequently integrated with various intelligence algorithms a method for finding numerous Pareto-optimal answers to a multi-objective problem.

As previously stated, the peer-to-peer network can be seen as a graph. Each node's location the x and y axes of the graph indicate it coordinate values, identifiable by its unique node number. If the Euclidian distance between two nodes is within each other, a node is said to be in the range of another node. Paths are recorded between clusters rather than between nodes in hierarchical routing, reducing routing control overhead. MMSA determines the smallest number of route path nodes. This is an iterative process, and the result is a temporary solution.

The process can be represented as follows:

```
Initialize each node

Initialize algorithm parameters

Create the initial population

Calculate each person's objective function values.

Filter the non-dominated solutions and record them into the external file Q

While (condition not met)

Iterate i to n times
```

Modify the locations of population individual

Perform the random movement on the non-dominated individuals

Choose ith node as a routing path

Modify the external file Q

Choose neighbor with maximum probability as next node routing path until all nodes are covered

Determine the final set of routing path nodes with maximum probability

4.7 SECURITY USING MODIFIED DOUBLE KEY ENCRYPTION

Attack prevention is ensured by introducing the Modified Double key encryption procedure to be encrypted before transmission.

Random value Generation: Each node generates a random number transmitted with the cluster head to complete the authentication process during this phase. A random number generator (RNG) creates a series of numbers or symbols that cannot be anticipated. A hardware random-number generator (HRNG) creates precise random numbers. A pseudo-random number generator (PRNG) creates random numbers that appear deterministic and can be repeated if the PRNG's state is known. A PRNG uses a seed state to start with an unspecified beginning state. Many numbers are generated quickly and replicated if the beginning stage in the sequence is known.

The programmers identified a method to introduce randomness into a computer program. Therefore, it is tough to persuade a computer to perform something randomly because it blindly follows the provided instructions and is thus fully predictable.

The generator is described by a recurrence relation:

$$Xn+1 = (aXn + c) \bmod c \qquad (4.10)$$

In which X denotes sequence of pseudo-random values

m, 0< m- modulus

a, 0< a <m- multiplier

c, 0< = c<m- increment

x0, 0<=x0<m- the seed or start value

The next random integer is generated using the preceding random numbers, the integer constants, and the modulus. To begin, the process requires an initial Seed. Performing modulo arithmetic creates the appearance of randomness. In this case, the randomly generated The modulus, the integer constants, and the previous random numbers are used to create the next random integer.

Secret Key Generation: Assume that X is a symmetric key or the random value supplied to a generator of asymmetric key pairs that has been validated. X must represent a bit string value represented as below:

$$X = U \oplus V \qquad (4.11)$$

- U denotes bit string of desired length
- V denotes bit string of similar length as U, and
- The value of V is detected as an independent value of U.

The process utilizes X to define needed bit length and minimum security strength. Since the process used to pick U provides most (if not all) of the requisite entropy, a conservative approach implies assuming that the mechanism used to select V provides the same. To put it another way, understanding one of the numbers (U or V) does not provide any information that can be used to understanding the other value (V). Here are some instances of independently derived V values, assuming U is a PRNG output:

1. The constant is V. (chosen independently from U). K = U, or the PRNG output, is the result if V is a sequence of binary zeros.

2. V is a key obtained using a key-derivation method with additional input that is not reliant on U;

3. V is independently created in other cryptographic modules and was secured by a key-wrapping algorithm or transferred by an approved key transport technique. When it is received, the key-generating module that made U before integrating V with U removes the protection on V.

4. V is created by hashing another bit string (V ') and shortening the result before combining it with U. V = T(H(V '), k) where T(x, k) displays x's k leftmost bits and k signifies U's length. The bit string V ' can be a) a constant; b) a key obtained from a shared secret in an approved key agreement mechanism between the key-generating module and another cryptographic module; or c) a key created independently by another module, ii) forwarded using an approved key wrapping algorithm or transferred using an approved key transport scheme, and iii) with its protection removed upon receipt.

4.7.1 First Level Encryption

In this work, we present an enhanced cryptosystem that encrypts the message using the RSA cryptosystem. To decrypt the message, the hacker must know the super-increasing sequence, the private key, and the public key. The data packet is first broken down into individual characters, converted to their binary counterparts. These characters are then encoded, completing the RSA encryption pattern. The primary idea is to generate a subset challenging that can be easily deciphered and then conceal the super-increasing nature by modular multiplication and variation. Additionally, these encoded characters are encoded using discrete logarithmic based on RSA concepts.

4.7.2 Second Level Encryption

The second level of encryption is performed using an upgraded AES algorithm with an increased number of rounds from 10 to 16 to enhance cryptographic complexity. The Polybius square was used to generate the first key. In AES, the encryption procedure includes the Sub bytes, ShiftRows, MixColumns, and AddRound Key operations. The suggested methodology's processing flow is depicted in Figure 4.2.

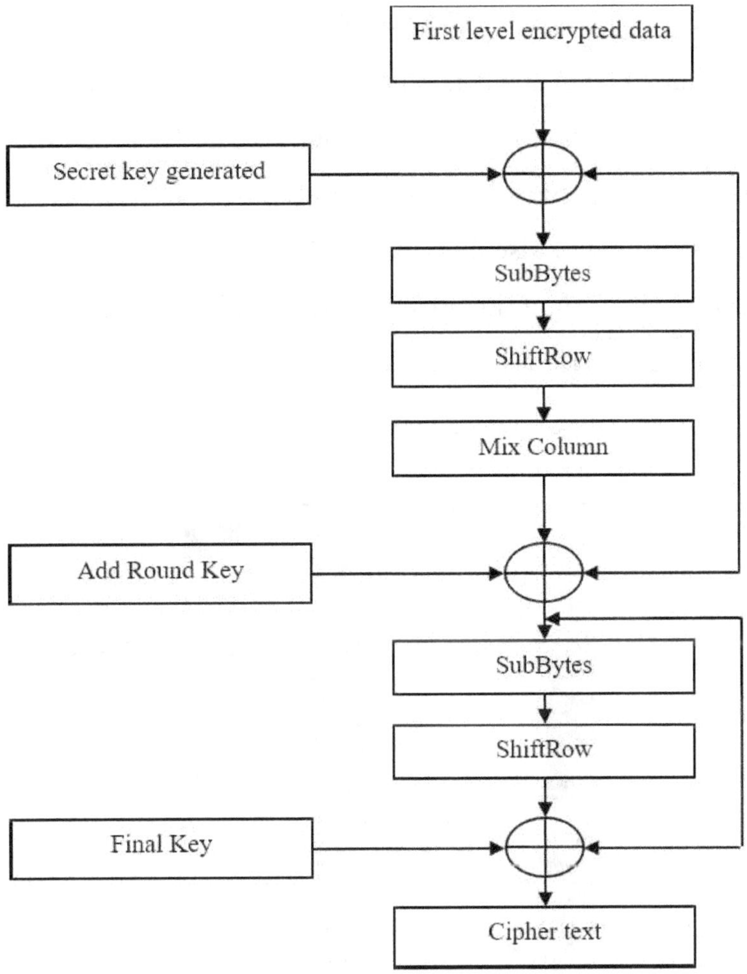

Figure 4.2 The processing flow of the improved AES algorithm

4.8 RESULTS AND DISCUSSION

The efficacy of collected information in the suggested methodology was evaluated using MATLAB environment.

Detection Rate, FARs , Precision, and Recall are just a few of the characteristics that have been used to assess the implementation of the solutions offered. The efficiency measurements listed below were discovered via modeling. The current techniques of TV-IDS, PCACID, and KBIDS have now been compared to the suggested CORF-IDS methodology. A variety of metrics are used to evaluate how well the processing operations are doing, and the bulk of them are based on the following four standards: True Positive (TP): Acceptance of the reality. False is appropriately identified as False in a True Negative (TN) statement. False Positive (FP): It is found to be true. False (correct identification) (right identification). Positive False: False is discovered (FN). Positive False (PN): False is discovered.

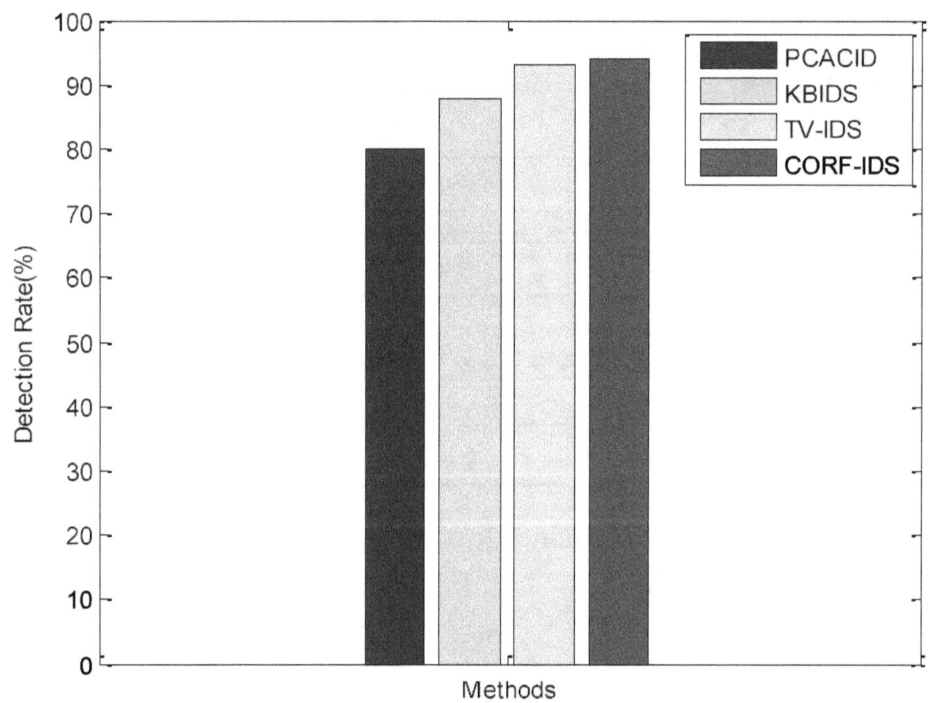

Figure 4.3 Detection rate comparison graph

Figure 4.3 displays the identification rate comparative chart, when a significant amount of attacking nodes, network data traffic, and unknown antigens have been processed via nodes. As a result, all three algorithms have increasing detection rates. Given the significant cost involved in using this approach to recognize nodes, it seems that the recommended CORF-IDS algorithm has a higher identification rate than other algorithms like PCACID, KBIDS, and TV-IDS.

FARs

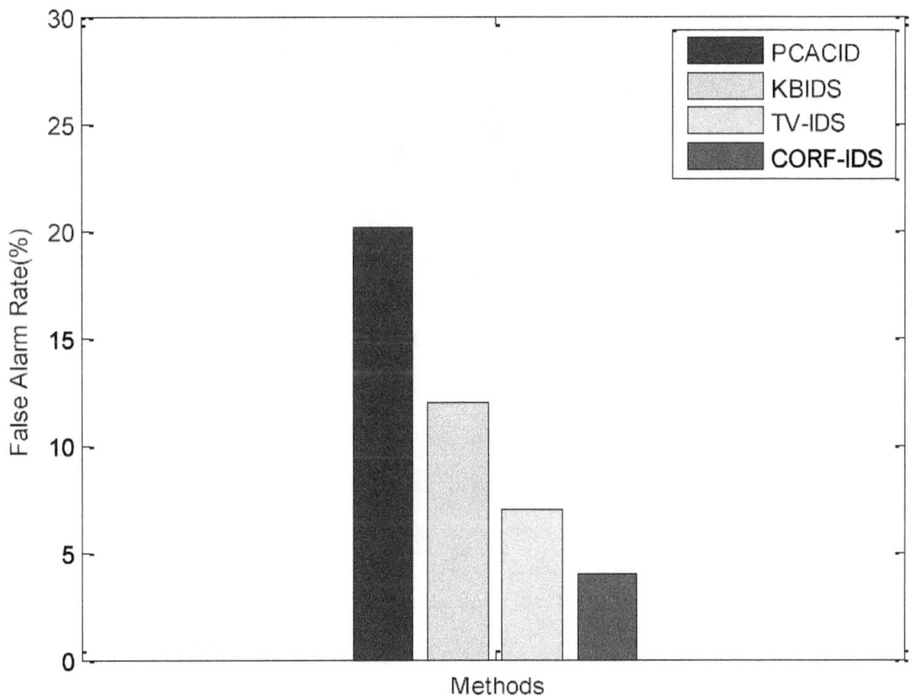

Figure 4.4 Comparative Graph of FARs

The outputs of the FARs are contrasted in Figure 4.4. The graph shows that, when compared to existing algorithms such as PCACID, KBIDS, and TV-IDS, the suggested CORF-IDS method gains a lower FARs value.

Precision

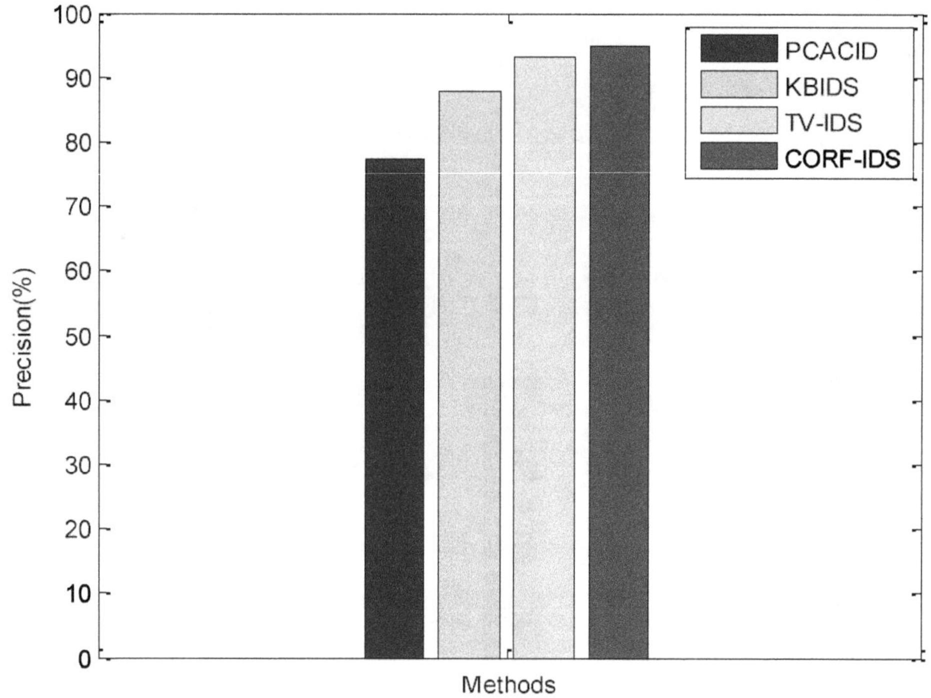

Figure 4.5 Precision comparison graph

The precision findings are analysed and compared in Figure 4.5, where it is shown that the recommended CORF-IDS method has a high Precision value when compared to other algorithms such as PCACID, KBIDS, and TV-IDS.

Recall

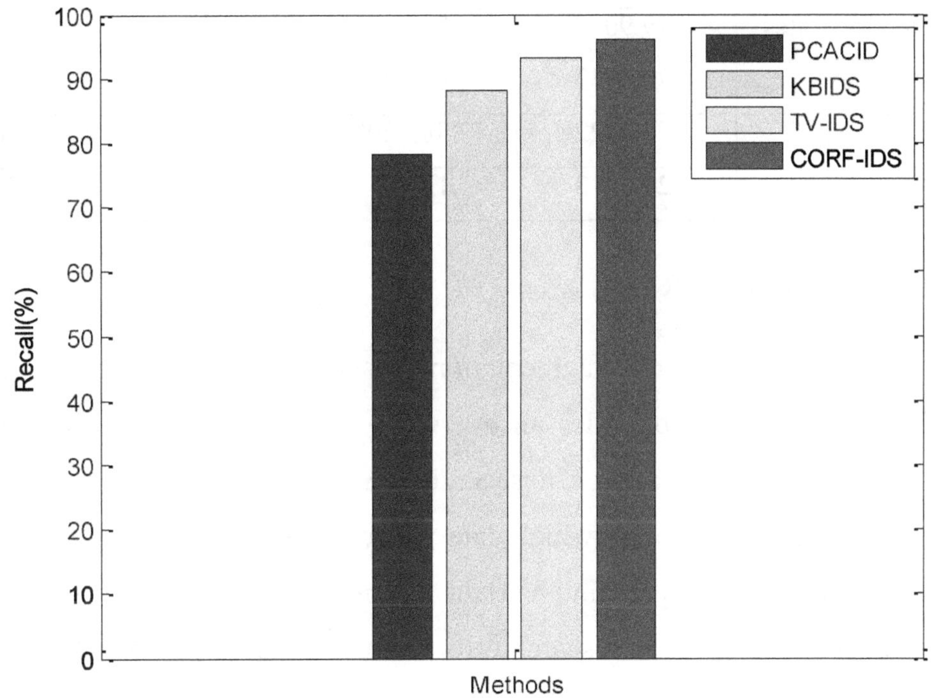

Figure 4.6 Recall comparison graph

Figure 4.6 shows a chart that compared the Recall by looking at the results. In which it is said that when compared to other algorithms such as PCACID, KBIDS, and TV-IDS, the suggested approach of CORF-IDS obtains the best recall rate.

The recommended techniques are thoroughly contrasted in Table 4.1 with regard to the crucial factors taken into account throughout the assessment process.

Table 4.1 Overall comparison of the parameters

Parameters	PCACID	KBIDS	TV-IDS	CORF-IDS
Detection Rates	79.9087	88	93	95
Precisions	77.3733	87.9752	92.9937	95
Recalls	78.0822	88.0208	92.9937	96
FARs	20.0913	12	7	4

4.9 SUMMARY

The idea of fragmentation attack detection is the aspect of this research, which provides an overview of secondary Server integration. This technique would place a secondary server between the receiver and transmitter nodes, through which data packets would be sent. In addition, as previously indicated, Bias and Variance estimate is performed to improve the overall processing of the research effort. Finally, the Truncated SVM method is used to learn about and anticipate the presence of an attack. The Modified Mosquito Swarm Algorithm selects the shortest route path to deliver the data packet with the least latency. The Modified Double key encryption process, which encrypts packets before transmission, ensures attack prevention.

CHAPTER 5

COMPUTATION OVERHEAD REDUCED, AND PRIVACY CONCERNED SECURED ROUTING IN WIRELESS SENSOR NETWORK

5.1 INTRODUCTION

In this research work, initially computation overhead of research work is reduced considerably by selecting the secondary server using modified squirrel search algorithm. Here user privacy is ensured along with secured routing by performing anonymous authentication of nodes in the chosen secondary server. After authentication, authenticated nodes are permitted for data transmission. Here optimal route path selection is done concern of trust metric using anarchy society optimization algorithm. The backup server is chosen in this operation utilizing modified squirrel search algorithm to ensure the computation overhead reduced processing.

5.2 COMPUTATION OVERHEAD REDUCED PRIVACY CONCERNED DATA TRANSMISSION

Due to the accessibility of inexpensive, short-range, and quickly deployable sensors, WSNs have expanded during the past several years (Khalaf & Sabbar 2019). Real-time data collection and transmission from a monitoring environment to a central server for further processing and analysis is the primary goal of WSN systems (Lee 2020).

Due to the increased exposure of wireless transmission in recent years' channels, concerns over safety and privacy in WSN systems have grown in popularity (Liu et al. 2020). This Special Issue aims to gather the most recent research on cutting-edge WSN system technologies, including the creation, development, testing, and implementation of service paradigms (Chen et al. 2022).

Wired and wireless networking, database management, and data mining have been examined extensively for privacy protection (Saleh et al. 2020). There are several fundamental characteristics of WSNs that make protecting privacy difficult in WSNs and exclude currently available approaches (Cao et al. 2020). Sensors may have to be put in an environment that the defence cannot control, such as a battlefield, allowing an opponent to undertake physical attacks to seize sensor nodes or deploy fraudulent ones (Chehri & Mouftah 2020).

For multiuser applications, some devices can synchronize without the need for an internet connection (Landaluce et al. 2020). Algorithms to improve accuracy utilize them to find the precise position. The Sybil attacker deceives other nodes in the wireless sensor network by displaying incorrect or duplicate IDs for users aware of the nodes' existence. Alien nodes might seem like original nodes in the most current network environment, taking on a variety of identities to fool users. There is no single controller node in the social and defence networks for intense monitoring of transmission between network nodes (Agbeboaye et al. 2018).

An unguided transmission channel (such as in a wireless network) makes wireless networks more vulnerable than wired networks in terms of safety threads (Kuo et al. 2018). When it comes to Wireless Sensor Networks (WSN), things get much more complicated because of the architectural differences. A command node or base station (a centralized entity) is common in WSNs (Lee 2020). While this may make things a little easier, the fundamental issue is with the nodes and the resource limitations on these low-cost sensors.

One of the most important and basic problems with wireless transmission channels is maintaining the safety and privacy of the WSN. Encryption/decryption and a digital signature mechanism are often used to prevent transmission data from being eavesdropped on, manipulated, or forged by unlawful nodes. Authentication is also a fundamental problem. Authentication techniques are commonly used to prevent unauthorized nodes from accessing the network's resources. We've devised a slew of protection methods to make our sensing network last longer. Still, they can't be too complicated because battery capacity on the sensing nodes is restricted.

These studies have as their primary objective the establishment of secure and private data transfer in a real-world context. This is accomplished in the suggested study by introducing a mechanism that utilizes a secondary server to authenticate users anonymously. Safety can be ensured while reducing computational overhead by providing that anonymous user authentication is possible.

5.3 SECONDARY SERVER SELECTION USING MODIFIED SQUIRREL SEARCH ALGORITHM

The initial processing overhead of this research study is significantly decreased in this work by picking the secondary server utilizing a modified squirrel search method. User privacy and secure routing are ensured by performing anonymous authentication of nodes in the chosen secondary server. Authenticated nodes are allowed to transmit data after authentication. The anarchic society optimization technique chooses the best route path from the metric trust perspective is depicted in Figure 5.1.

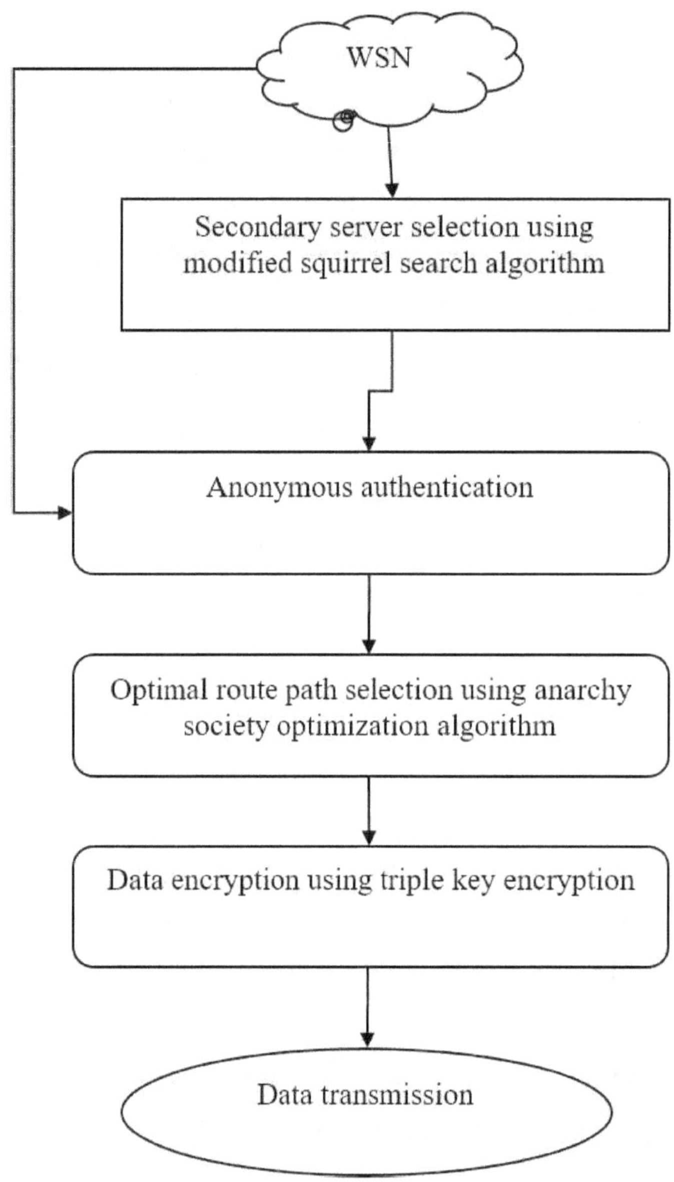

Figure 5.1 The processing flow of suggested work

The secondary server selection algorithm used here is a modified squirrel search algorithm to reduce processing time. The general squirrel search algorithm is based on flying squirrel food foraging. The algorithm's primary purpose is to discover the best food sources for flying squirrels. The squirrel search technique seems to take longer to compute and anticipate the ideal answer. The modified squirrel search algorithm adds the Gbest parameter to the standard. Instead of updating positions randomly, the suggested modified squirrel search algorithm finds Gbest for every solution. Therefore, the algorithm will find the best secondary server for anonymous node authentication.

Algorithm: Secondary server selection using modified squirrel search algorithm

Input: WSN nodes

Output: Secondary server

1: Begin

2: Do

3: Initialize the population

Initialize the location

LSi = (LSi1, LSi2,…,LSid)

where i=1,2,…,n

LSij = jth location of ith squirrel

n= population

$$d_g = \frac{h_g}{\tan(\varphi) \times sf} \tag{5.1}$$

Where dg → Gliding distance

hg → constant value = 8

sf → constant value = 18

$$\tan(\varphi) = \frac{D}{L} \tag{5.2}$$

Where tan (φ)→ gliding angle

D → drag force

L → Lift force

$$D = \frac{1}{2\rho V^2 S C_D} \tag{5.3}$$

$$L = \frac{1}{2\rho V^2 S C_L} \tag{5.4}$$

Where ρ→ constant =1.204 kg m-3

V → constant = 5.25 ms-1

S → 154 cm2

CD → constant = 0.6

CL → random number between 0.675 and 1.5

4: For each individual in population

5: Find the fitness value (Classification accuracy)

6: Find the Gbest value

If (bestFit > Fit)

Update bestFit as Gbest

Else

Update Fit as Gbest

7: Update the position of parameters based on Gbest value

If **r** > P_{dp}

$LS_i + i = LS_i + d_g \times G_c \times (Ft_h - LS)_i$

If (fitness of current squirrel < Gbest)

LSi = LSL + U(0,1) x Gbest (LSu LSL)

Else

Choose random location

End IF

End IF

Where

LSL and LSU = lower and upper bounds of squirrel

8: End for

9: If all individuals' position is not updated

10: Go to step 3

11: Else

12: Find the best parameter values based on Gbest value

13: Find the seasonal transitional judgment and Update the position of individual

$$S_c^t = \sqrt{\sum_{k[1}^{D}(F_{ai,k}^t - F_{h,k}^t)^2} \quad i = 1,2, \ldots, Nf_s \tag{5.5}$$

$$S_{min} = \frac{10e^{-6}}{(365)^{\frac{t}{T}} 2.5}$$

Where T amount of iteration

If < Smin

Winter over and season turns to summer

Else

Season unchanged

End if

If season = summer and present in fh

Stay at the previously updated position

Else if season =summer and present in fa

Update the position as like in below eq

$$LS_{inew}^{t+1} = LS_L + \mathbf{Levy(n)} \times (LS_U - LS_L)$$

Where Levy → random walk model

$$\text{Levy}(x) = 0.01 \times \frac{r_a \times \sigma}{|r_b|^{1/\beta}}$$

Where β→ constant = 1.5

$$\sigma = \left(\frac{\Gamma(1+\beta) \times \sin(\frac{\pi\beta}{2})}{\Gamma\left(\frac{1+\beta}{2}\right) \times \beta \times 2^{\left(\frac{\beta-1}{2}\right)}} \right)^{\frac{1}{\beta}}$$

where $\Gamma(x) = (x-1)!$

14: End if

15: Repeat till convergence reached

16: End

The algorithm mentioned above will outcome in the optimum selected secondary server. In addition, this specified secondary server will perform anonymous authentication, leading to computation overhead reduced protected data transfer.

5.4 ANONYMOUS AUTHENTICATION

Two-factor authentication solutions for WSNs must ensure the anonymity of their users. Such an advanced property can be achieved by a method that prevents users' transmissions from being linked to each other and from being traced back to their location or moving history. Therefore, most plans to protect user privacy strive to achieve this higher level of anonymity for users. This work's anonymous authentication procedure is depicted in the following characteristics:

- Configuration of the registration phase, during which all members of the cluster communicate their temporal identity with the cluster head
- Other nodes can't figure out the cluster's temporal identity because it's created randomly by each cluster member.
- The cluster leader will create the secret key using this temporal identity and divide it into two shares.
- The proper cluster member will get the first share in this instance, and the secondary cluster leader will receive the second share.
- Therefore, no node can recognize other users' personal data.
- This confidential data will be used in the authentication procedure.

5.4.1 Random Value Generation Phase

Each node in the environment creates a random number at this point. a machine that generates random numbers (RNG) produces a series of numbers or symbols that can only be predicted randomly. Actual random number generators are available hardware RNG (HRNG) or pseudo-RNG (PRNG), which create numbers that appear random but are predictable and can be repeated if the PRNG's state is known. A PRNG generates a set of numbers that closely resemble the characteristics of random numbers. As a result, big numbers may be generated fast and repeated later if the beginning of the series is known. As a result, the data is trustworthy and predictable.

After computers were created, programmers recognised they needed a mechanism to include randomness into computer code. Nevertheless, as absurd as it may sound, getting a computer to accomplish anything is challenging. Because it mindlessly follows the given commands and is completely predictable, it behaves arbitrarily. Consequently, PRNG is a method created to generate random numbers. One must use a computer to generate numbers since it is challenging to manufacture random numbers from predictable objects like computers.

The Linear Congruential Generator is the most popular and straightforward method for generating pseudo-random numbers. The generator is defined by the recurring relationship as follows:

$$Xn+1 = (aXn + c) \bmod c \tag{5.6}$$

In which X is the sequence of pseudo-random values

m, 0< m- modulus

a, 0< a <m- multiplier

c, 0< = c<m- increment

x0, 0<=x0<m- the seed or start value

Incorporating the prior random number, integer constants, and integer modulus, we create the next random integer. To begin, the method involves the initial Seed. Implementing modulo arithmetic creates the impression of randomness. In this case, the randomly created for a subsequent action, number will be switched with the cluster head.

$$\text{Node} \xRightarrow{\text{PRNG } X_{n+1}} \text{ClusterHead} \tag{5.7}$$

5.4.2 Secret Key Generation and Sharing Phase

Assume that X is a symmetric key or a random number that is used as input to a procedure that is permitted to generate asymmetric key pairs. X is the specified bit string value of the following sequence:

$$X = U \oplus V \tag{5.8}$$

- U is the result of an approved PRNG and is a bit string of the specified length managing the needed safety strength to safeguard the target data,
- V is a bit string of the equal length as U, and
- The acquisition of the value of V isolates it from the value of U.

The algorithm and safety strength X will be used to determine the needed bit length and minimum safety strength. Since the method used to select U gives most (if not all) of the needed entropy, a conservative strategy implies the same for V., To put it another way, knowing one of the numbers (U or V) offers no knowledge about the other (V). Examples of independently obtained V values for U, presuming U is a PRNG outcome:

- The constant is V. (chosen uniquely from the value of U). Keep in mind that if V is a series of binary zeroes, then K Equals U, or the result of a permitted PRNG.

- A critical derivation key and additional input that are distinct from U are used to derive the key V using a key-derivation procedure;

- A key generated specifically for another cryptographic unit is called V. During future transfer, V was protected using an approved key-wrapping algorithm or carried using an allowed critical transport process. Upon reception, the key-generating mechanism created U before integrating V with U Removes V's protection.

- Another bit string (V ') is hashed using an approved hash function to form V, which is then combined with U after, if required, being truncated to the right length. Meaning that V = T (H (V '), k), where k is the length of U and T (x, k) denotes the truncation of bit string x to its k leftmost bits. The bit string V ' may be a constant, a key obtained from a shared secret between the key-generating unit and another cryptographic unit, or a key generated by a different unit, delivered using a key wrapping method or transferred using a key transport mechanism, and then secured upon receipt.

5.4.3 Authentication Phase

Secret Sharing is based on Adi Shamir's private sharing method. It's a type of personal sharing when a secret is divided into parts and given to each participant. Functions are needed to recreate the original secret. This amount is less than the total amount of pieces. Otherwise, everyone must rebuild the actual secret. The Secret of Shamir Spreading a secret is done by sharing, generally to protect other encryption keys. Shares of the secret have been split. These shares aid in putting the first puzzle together. A minimum amount of shares is needed to open Shamir's secret sharing. The threshold is the minimum amount of shares necessary to unlock the secret.

Divide secret S (for example, a safe's combination) into n data S1,..., Sn so that:

- Knowing k or more Si pieces simplifies S. That is, any k data points can reconstruct the entire secret S.

- Knowledge of any k-1 or less Si pieces leaves S entirely indeterminate, in that the different values for S are equally likely as knowing zero pieces. Alternatively, with less than k pieces, the secret S cannot be constructed.

The (k,n) threshold mechanism. Every component of the initial secret S is required if k=n.

It is created by our effort and shared with the associated node and secondary server. These secret shares will be compared during data transmission and an authentication choice taken based on the outcome.

5.5 OPTIMAL ROUTE PATH SELECTION USING ANARCHY SOCIETY OPTIMIZATION ALGORITHM

The anarchic society optimization technique is used to determine the ideal travel path. Finally, the route path construction node is chosen based on trust values.

5.5.1 Trust Level Estimation

Trust can be expressed as a continuous variable (-1 to +1) or as discrete values (low, medium, high, extremely high). As soon as a node in the network receives a transmission request from another node, it begins determining the requesting node's trust value. This is referred to as the node's indirect trust value. The node's initial degree of trust is represented by the indirect trust value. The node begins communicating if its initial trust value is adequate for transmission. If not, it's a simple value-trust assessment. The three models of safety, mobility, and dependability used in the trust framework are also used in the direct trust evaluation.

Algorithm: For Computing the Trust of the Node.

Pre-conditions: The network's nodes must communicate with one another as a precondition.

Inputs: Node-id, safety, dependability, and mobility

Outputs: The computation and sharing of trust values.

Begin:

Initial node trust calculation:

If the initial is sufficient for transmission, allow transmission with the node.
Initial = (S+U)/ (Ti+S) or Pr.

Alternately, calculate the node's confidence in the safety model.

If Ts=A+E+R (Ts is enough for transmission)

Then permit transmissions with nodes.

Else calculate trust values for node's mobility model

If nodes are consistent

Then consider node trust values in mobility models as zero.

Else calculate trust values of nodes in mobility

Tm=Me+Em;

If (Tm is enough for the transmission)

Then allow the transmission with node.

Else compute the trust for the node in the reliability model.

Tr=D+Ed ;

If (Tr is enough for transmission)

Then permit transmission;

Else calculate complete trusts for nodes.

Entire trust=Tinitial+Ts+Tm+Tr;

If Complete trusts are enough for transmissions

Then permit transmissions with nodes.

Else

Disallow transmissions with nodes

End.

5.5.2 Route Path Construction Using Anarchy Society Optimization

The Anarchic Society algorithm is ideological. The ASO algorithm states that members of a society change viewpoints based on individual, group, syndicate experiences, and past societal experiences. Sooner or later, one of the society's members will attain a near-ideal position. In this work, N people hunt for the most ACCEPTABLE place to reside in an unknown area. Xi (k) is the ith member's position at the kth iteration, and Gbest is the ith member's best position at the first k iterations. The initialized solution will use a random selection of members. The position update will be dependent on each member's fitness value. Then the local and global best values will be chosen. This is continued for n iterations until convergence.

Each characteristic is a community member with a fitness value in this research. Each feature's correlation is calculated in terms of data gain. The entropy parameter helps determine each feature's data gain. The following equation shows how to calculate data.

$$\text{Entropy of X: } H(X) = -\sum P\,(x_i)\log_2(P(x_i)) \qquad (5.9)$$

Entropy of X based on observed Y: H (X/Y) =

$$-\sum P(y_i)\sum P\left({}^{X_i}/_{y_j}\right)\log_2(P({}^{X_i}/_{y_j})) \qquad (5.5)$$

In which P(xi) → prior probability of X

P (xi/yj) → posterior probabilities of X with given Y values

Data Gain of X with given Y:

$$IG(X/Y) = H(X).\,H(X/Y) \qquad (5.10)$$

The fitness function taken from equation 13 reduces the amount of features. Less associated features will be filtered for further processing. This fitness value will optimize the anarchic society optimization algorithm for feature retrieval.

The algorithm of ASO for feature retrieval is:

Algorithm: Feature retrieval using ASO

Input: Acquired feature vectors from CNN

Output: Reduced feature vectors

1: Begin

2: Set the population (set of features) randomly

3: Determine the fitness value of every population

4: Recognize the Pbest and Gbest as per computed fitness value

5: If previous feature best values are close to present location

6: Allocate the present population of features to the following location

7: Else

8: Allocate the randomly chosen population of features to the next position

9: End if

10: If evaluated fitness is an equation to Pbest

11: Allocate the present population of feature as Pbest value

12: Else

13: Allocate the randomly chosen population of feature Pbest value

14: End if

15: If evaluated fitness is an equation to Gbest

16: Allocate the present population of feature as Gbest value

17: Else

18: Allocate the randomly chosen population of feature Gbest value

19: End if

20: Carryout Crossover and mutation on a chosen population of features

21: Recognize the fitness of a population

22: If attained optimization criteria

23: Stop

24: Else

25: Go to step 4

26: End If

The approach described above generates an optimized feature set vector and sends it to the suggested classifier for DR forecasting.

5.6 DATA ENCRYPTION USING TRIPLE LEVEL ENCRYPTION

In this work, cross over mutation integrated three level encryption is introduced for improvising the security level. Here first level and second level encryption is done as like in our previous work. In the first level encryption RSA cryptosystem is utilized and for the second level encryption AES algorithm is utilized. The outcome obtained from the double encryption is send to the cross over and mutation process. The goal of this step is to disperse the encrypted blocks produced by the AES and Feistel encryptions.

The genetic algorithm includes the cross over and mutation methods. In the cross over process, two blocks are randomly modified while being changed jointly. Cross over begins by selecting the cross over spots at random for two blocks. For the purpose of decryption, these points are noted and saved. The blocks starting at the cross over locations and ending at the least significant bit are then switched. As an example, take the two blocks 010100101011 and 100101010101. The resultant blocks are: 010100100101 and 100101011011 if the cross over point is 8.

In a genetic algorithm, the mutations process is employed to preserve the general variety of outputs in a random manner from one iteration to the next. The mutation procedure begins by randomly choosing one mutation site for each of two blocks. The mutations point is recorded for the decryption process at each block, where the bit relating to it is flip-flopped. The mutation procedure for the two blocks 010100101011 and 100101010101 is an example. The two blocks that arise if the recombination point is 8 are 010100100011 and 100101011101.

There are several repetitions of the crossover and mutation procedures. We do these actions five times in our studies. At this point, the encrypted 256-bit chunk, the cross over points, and the mutation points are the only pieces of encrypted data that need to be transferred to the recipient. The processing flow of the proposed encryption method is shown below:

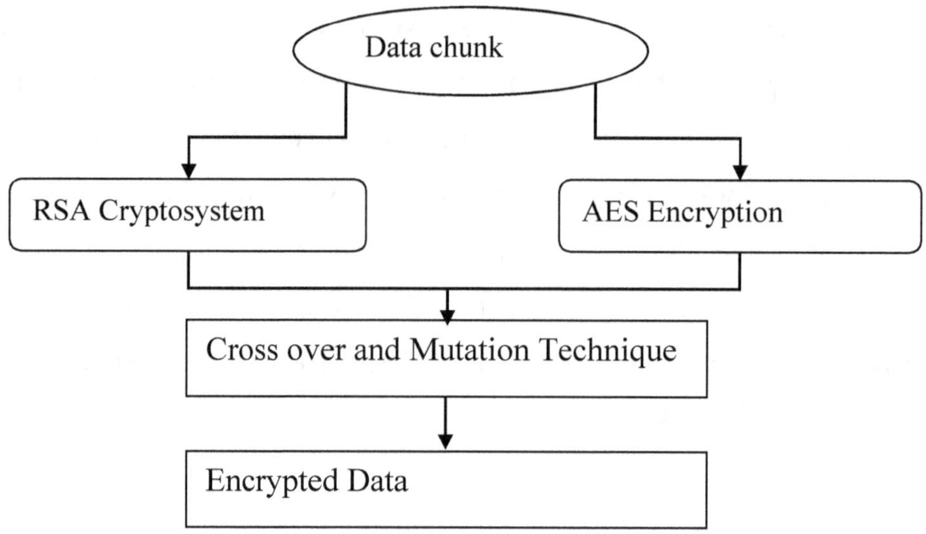

Figure 5.2 Three Level Encryption

5.7 RESULTS AND DISCUSSION

The recommended approaches' effectiveness was evaluated empirically in MATLAB. The BS was placed in the centre of a network architecture of heterogeneous nodes with initial energies ranging from 0.5J to 2.25J. Therefore, each protocol's average power usage is guaranteed to be similar at 102.5J. Moreover, applying these protocols' more acceptable parameters has increased their efficiency.

The effectiveness of the offered strategies was evaluated using Detection Rates, FARs, Precisions, and Recalls. In addition, the following performance indicators were determined using simulation. Now, COR-PCDT is compared to CORF-IDS, TV-IDS, PCACID, and KBIDS. The performance of the techniques is determined by several measurements, which rely on four parameters, i.e. Recognized accurate False (correct determination), True Negative (TN): False Positive (FP): True is determined. False Negative (FN): YES (incorrect determination).

Detection rate

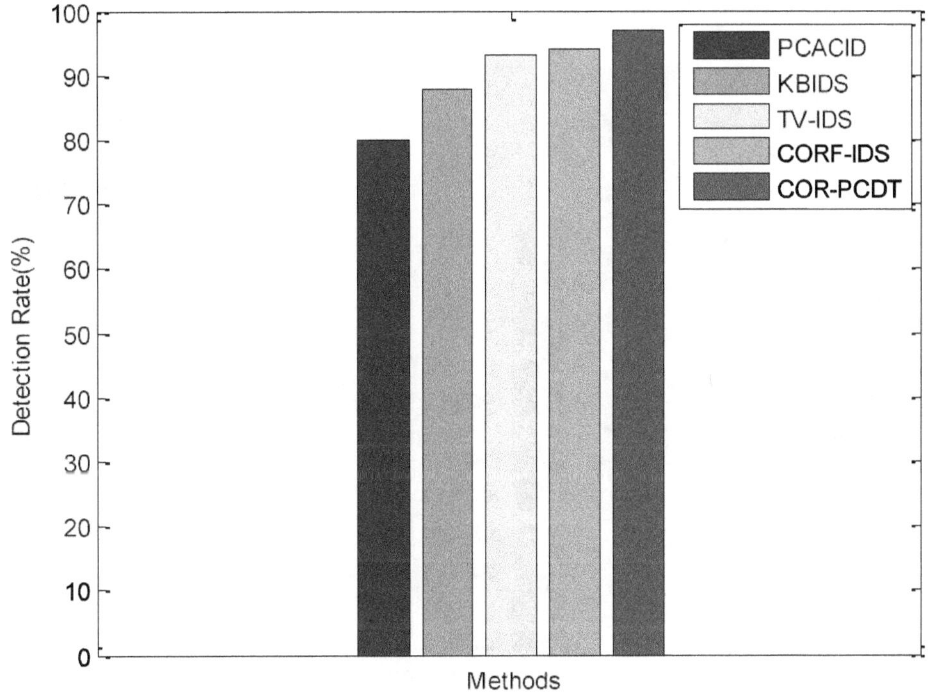

Figure 5.3 Detection rate comparison graph

Figure 5.3 shows the detection rate comparison chart after a significant amount of attacking nodes, network data traffic, and unknown antigens have been processed through nodes. As a result, all three algorithms have increasing detection rates. Given the significant cost involved in using this approach to identify nodes, it appears that the recommended COR-PCDT technique has a higher detection rate when compared to algorithms like CORF-IDS, PCACID, KBIDS, and TV-IDS.

FARs

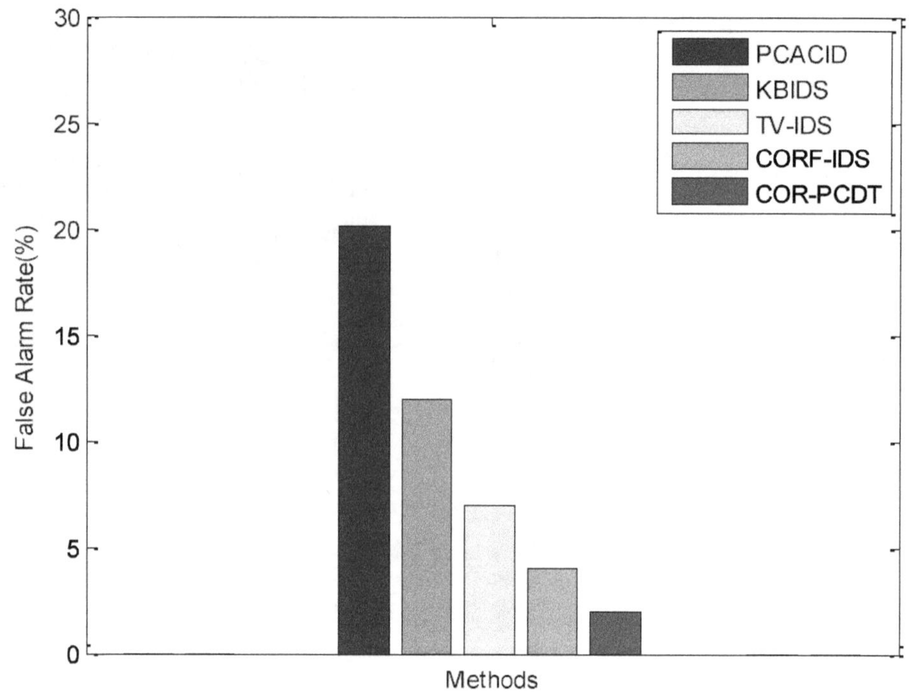

Figure 5.4 Comparative Graph of FARs

The outputs of the FARs are contrasted in Figure 5.4. The graph shows that, when compared to other algorithms such as CORF-IDS, PCACID, KBIDS, and TV-IDS, the suggested method of COR-PCDT gains a lower value of FARs.

Precision

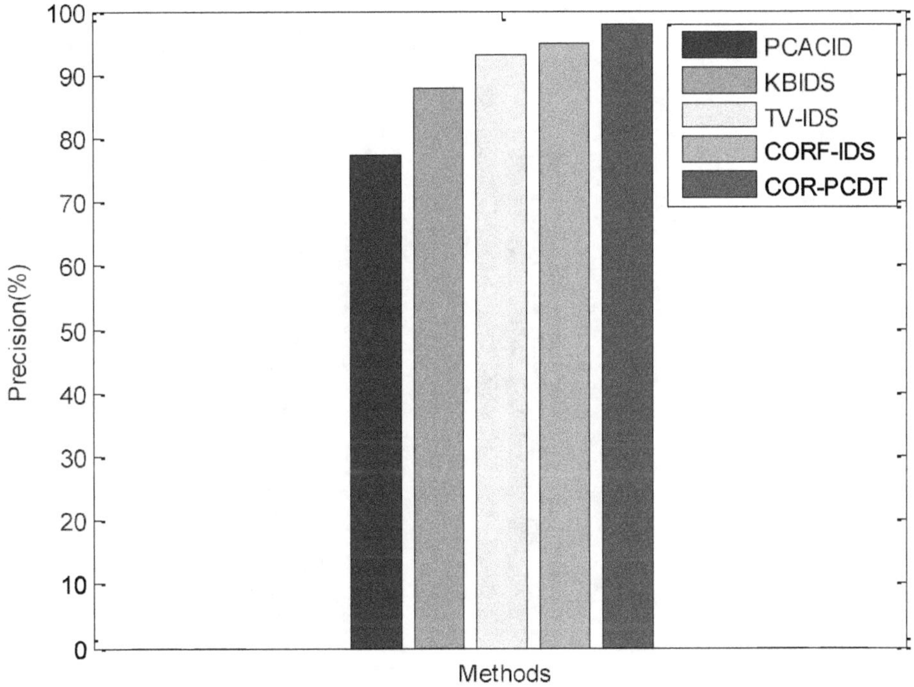

Figure 5.5 Precision comparison graph

The precision findings are analysed and compared in Figure 5.5, where it is shown that the recommended COR-PCDT method has a high Precision value when compared to other algorithms such as CORF-IDS, PCACID, KBIDS, and TV-IDS.

Recall

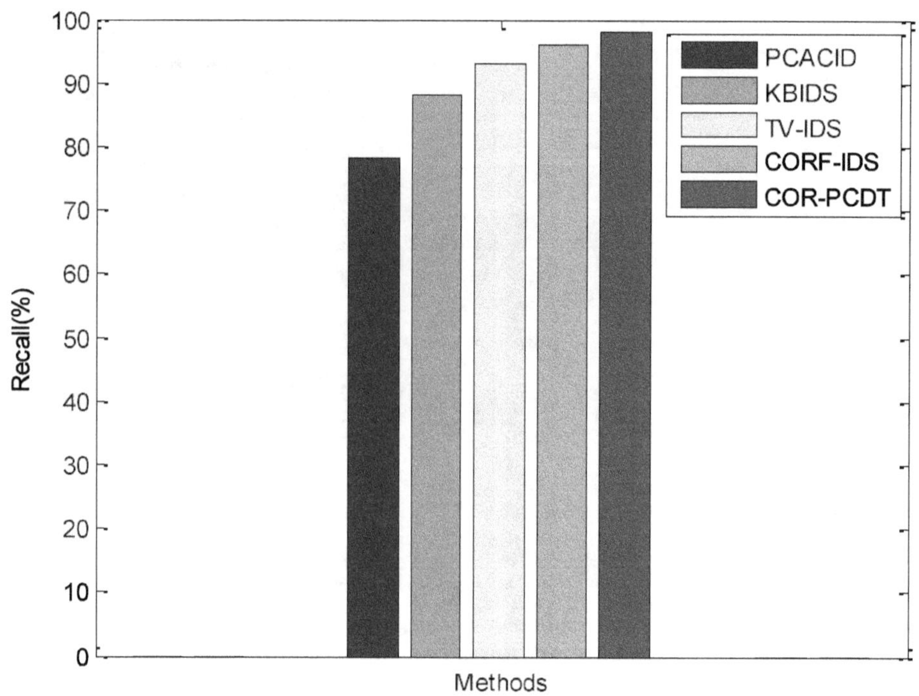

Figure 5.6 Recall comparison graph

Figure 5.6 shows a chart that compared the Recall by looking at the results. In which it is said that when compared to other algorithms such as CORF-IDS, PCACID, KBIDS, and TV-IDS, the suggested approach of COR-PCDT obtains the best recall rate.

The recommended techniques are thoroughly contrasted in Table 5.1 with regard to the crucial factors taken into account throughout the assessment process.

Table 5.1 Overall comparison of the parameters

Parameters	PCACID	KBIDS	TV-IDS	CORF-IDS	COR-PCDT
Detection Rate	79.9087	88	93	95	97
Precision	77.3733	87.9752	92.9937	95	98
Recall	78.0822	88.0208	92.9937	96	98
FARs	20.0913	12	7	4	2

5.8 SUMMARY

This study lowered the initial computational overhead by using the Modified squirrel search method to select the secondary server. User privacy and secure routing are ensured by performing anonymous authentication of nodes in the chosen secondary server. Authenticated nodes are allowed to transmit data after authentication. The anarchic society optimization technique chooses the best route path in light of the trust metric. Finally, triple key encryption method is employed to make sure the comprehensive analysis of the research effort is performed in the MATLAB simulation environment, and it is demonstrated that the suggested method outperforms the traditional approaches.

A CERTAIN INVESTIGATION ON INTRUSION DETECTION SYSTEM FOR ENSURING SECURED DATA TRANSMISSION IN WIRELESS SENSOR NETWORK

A THESIS

Submitted by

PRABHU T N

in partial fulfillment of the requirements for the degree of

DOCTOR OF PHILOSOPHY

FACULTY OF INFORMATION AND COMMUNICATION ENGINEERING

ANNA UNIVERSITY

CHENNAI 600 025

APRIL 2023

CHAPTER 6

CONCLUSION AND FUTURE WORK

6.1 CONCLUSION

One of the primary concerns that should be carefully considered in wireless sensor networks in order to identify secure and reliable data processing is intruder attack. The various characteristics of incursion threats should be precisely adjusted because they have an impact on the dependability of the intruder detecting outcomes. For the process of clustering feature, the first study effort provided a mean-shift clustering based on fuzzy technique, with the perfect clustering output accompanied by the decreased complexity of time. In this work, the bias variation of the data points has been estimated before being fed into the decision classifier. Minor traffic variations won't result in anomalous data based on the value of variance. In addition to the genetic algorithm's assistance in modifying and selecting the ANFIS weight values in an ideal manner, a hybrid genetic neuro-fuzzy classifier for the classification process has been proposed in this study. Finally, the Artificial Bee Colony algorithm selected the best route to go. Second research work focused on the idea of fragmentation attack detection which provides an overview of secondary Server integration. This technique would place a secondary server between the receiver and transmitter nodes, through which data packets would be sent. In addition, as previously indicated, Bias and Variance estimate is performed to improve the overall processing of the research effort. Finally, the Truncated SVM method is used to learn about and anticipate the presence of an attack.

The Modified Mosquito Swarm Algorithm selects the shortest route path to deliver the data packet with the least latency. T he Modified Double key encryption process, which encrypts packets before transmission, ensures attack prevention.In the third research work, initially computation overhead of research work is reduced considerably by selecting the secondary server using Modified squirrel search algorithm. Here user privacy is ensured along with secured routing by performing anonymous authentication of nodes in the chosen secondary server. After authentication, authenticated nodes are permitted for data transmission. Here optimal route path selection is done concern of trust metric using anarchy society optimization algorithm. The Matlab simulation environment is used to carry out the entire examination of the technical job, and it reveals that the suggested technique achieves superior performance than the existing methodologies.

6.2 FUTURE WORK

Future works will highlight on introducing and testing other extensions to improve the meta heuristics techniques for feature selection issues typically, and the intrusion detection system especially. The m/More parameters can be determined for network features to boost threat detecting effectiveness. Future work involves validating the system with actual network data. The real time data can be produced and gathered using different attack simulation tools, which can provide coverage for several novel attack specifications.

REFERENCES

1. Agbeboaye, C, Akpojedje, FO & Okoekhian, J 2018, 'Security threats area network,' Compusoft, vol. 7, no. 6, pp. 2773-2779.

2. Ahmad, B, Jian, W, Enam, RN & Abbas, A 2021, 'Classification of DoS attacks in smart underwater wireless sensor network,' Wireless Personal Communications, vol. 116, no. 2, pp. 1055-1069.

3. Ali, MH, Al Mohammed, BAD, Ismail, A & Zolkipli, MF 2018, 'A new intrusion detection system based on fast learning network and particle swarm optimization,' IEEE Access, vol. 6, pp. 20255-20261.

4. Aljawarneh, S, Aldwairi, M & Yassein, MB2018,'Anomaly-based intrusion detection system through feature selection analysis and building hybrid efficient model,' Journal of Computational Science, vol. 25, pp. 152-160.

5. Almomani, I, Al-Kasasbeh, B & Al-Akhras, M 2016, 'WSN-DS: A dataset for intrusion detection systems in wireless sensor networks,' Journal of Sensors, vol. 2016, no. 2 , pp. 1-16.

6. Alqahtani, M, Gumaei, A, Mathkour, H & Maher Ben Ismail, M 2019, 'A genetic-based extreme gradient boosting model for detecting intrusions in wireless sensor networks,' Sensors, vo. 19, no. 20, pp. 4383.

7. Al-Shaihk, NFA & Hassanpour, R 2019, 'Active defense strategy against jamming attack in wireless sensor networks,' International Journal of Computer Network and Information Security, vol. 9, no. 11, pp. 1-13.

8. Alsirhani, A, Bodorik, P & Sampalli, S 2017, 'Improving database security in cloud computing by fragmentation of data,' In 2017 International Conference on Computer and Applications (ICCA), pp. 43-49.

9. Amish, P & Vaghela, VB 2016,'Detection and prevention of wormhole attack in wireless sensor network using AOMDV protocol,' Procedia computer science, vol. 79, pp. 700-707.

10. Amouri, A, Morgera, S, Bencherif, M & Manthena, R 2018,'A Cross-Layer, Anomaly-Based IDS for WSN and MANET Sensors, vol. 18, no. 2, pp. 1-17.

11. Anwar, S, Mohamad Zain, J, Zolkipli, MF, Inayat, Z, Khan, S, Anthony, B & Chang, V 2017, From intrusion detection to an intrusion response system: fundamentals, requirements, and future directions,Algorithms, vol. 10, no. 2, pp. 39.

12. Apostolaki, M, Zohar, A & Vanbever, L 2017,'Hijacking bitcoin: Routing attacks on cryptocurrencies,' In 2017 IEEE Symposium on Security and Privacy (SP), pp. 375-392.

13. Athari, M & Borna, K 2016, 'Using Metaheuristic Algorithms of Genetic, Particle Swarm Optimization And Glowworm In The Intrusion Detection System,' International Journal of Computer Science and Network Security, vol. 16, no. 10, pp. 78-86.

14. Brinck, K, Fischer, R, Groeneveld, J, Lehmann, S, Dantas De Paula, M, Pütz, S, Sexton, JO, Song, D & Huth, A 2017, 'High resolution analysis of tropical forest fragmentation and its impact on the global carbon cycle,' Nature Communications, vol. 8, no. 1, pp. 1-6.

15. Butun, I, Morgera, SD & Sankar, R 2013,'A survey of intrusion detection systems in wireless sensor networks,' IEEE communications surveys and tutorials, vol. 16, no. 1, pp. 266-282.

16. Cao, L, Jiang, X, Zhao, Y, Wang, S, You, D & Xu, X 2020, 'A survey of network attacks on cyber-physical systems, 'IEEE Access, vol. 8, pp. 44219-44227.

17. Cepheli, Ö, Büyükçorak, S & Karabulut Kurt, G 2016, 'Hybrid intrusion detecton system for ddos attacks,' Journal of Electrical and Computer Engineering. vol. 2016, no. 1075648, pp. 1-8.

18. Chehri, A & Mouftah, HT 2020,'Internet of Things-integrated IR-UWB technology for healthcare applications,' Concurrency and Computation: Practice and Experience, vol. 32, no. 2, pp. e5454.

19. Chen, L, Liu, N & Wang, J 2020, 'Peer-to-peer energy sharing in distribution networks with multiple sharing regions,' IEEE Transactions on Industrial Informatics, vol. 16, no. 11, pp. 6760-6771.

20. Chen, Y , Sun, J , Yang, Y, Li, T, Niu, X & Zhou, H 2022, 'PSSPR: a source location privacy protection scheme based on sector phantom routing in WSNs,' International Journal of Intelligent Systems, vol. 37, no. 2, pp. 1204-1221.

21. Cheng, G, Guo, S, Yang, Y & Wang, F 2015, 'Replication attack detection with monitor nodes in clustered wireless sensor networks,' In 2015 IEEE 34th International Performance Computing and Communications Conference (IPCCC), pp. 1-8.

22. Choi, HB, Ko, YB & Lim, KW 2018, 'Energy-Aware Distribution of Data Fragments in Unattended Wireless Sensor Networks,' In 2018 Third International Conference on Security of Smart Cities, Industrial Control System and Communications (SSIC), pp. 1-8.

23. Cui, Y, Yan, L, Li, S, Xing, H, Pan, W, Zhu, J & Zheng, X 2016, 'SD-A nti-DDoS: Fast and efficient DDoS defense in software-defined networks,' J ournal of Network and Computer A pplications, vol. 68, pp. 65-79.

24. Deka, D, Baldick, R & Vishwanath, S 2016, 'Jamming aided data attacks: exposing vulnerabilities in secure estimation,' In 2016 49th Hawaii International Conference on System Sciences (HICSS), pp. 2556-2565.

25. Diro, AA, Chilamkurti, N & Nam, Y 2018, 'A nalysis of lightweight encryption scheme for fog-to-things communication,' IEEE Access, vol. 6, pp. 26820-26830.

26. Duan, J, Yang, D, Zhu, H, Zhang, S & Zhao, J 2014, 'TSRF: A trust-aware secure routing framework in wireless sensor networks,' International J ournal of Distributed Sensor Networks, vol. 2014, no. 209436, pp. 14.

27. Eesa, AS, Orman, Z & Brifcani, AMA 2015, 'A novel feature-selection approach based on the cuttlefish optimization algorithm for intrusion detection systems,' Expert systems with applications, vol. 42, no. 5, pp. 2670-2679.

28. Esquivel-Vargas, H, Caselli, M & Peter, A 2017,'Automatic deployment of specification-based intrusion detection in the BACnet protocol,' In Proceedings of the 2017 Workshop on Cyber-Physical Systems Security and PrivaCy, pp. 25-36.

29. Faheem, M, Abbas, MZ, Tuna, G & Gungor, VC 2015, 'EDHRP: Energy efficient event driven hybrid routing protocol for densely deployed wireless sensor networks,' Journal of network and computer applications, vol. 58, pp. 309-326.

30. Fotohi, R & Firoozi Bari, S 2020, 'A novel countermeasure technique to protect WSN against denial-of-sleep attacks using firefly and Hopfield neural network (HNN) algorithms,' The Journal of Supercomputing, vol. 76, no. 9, pp. 6860-6886.

31. Fotohi, R, Firoozi Bari, S & Yusefi, M2020,'Securing wireless sensor networks against denial-of-sleep attacks using RSA cryptography algorithm and interlock protocol,' International Journal of Communication Systems, vol. 33, no. 4, pp. e4234.

32. Fouchal, S, Mansouri, D, Mokdad, L & Iouallalen, M 2015,'Recursive-clustering-based approach for denial of service (DoS) attacks in wireless sensors networks,' International journal of communication systems, vol. 28, no. 2, pp. 309-324.

33. Ghaffari, A 2015,'Congestion control mechanisms in wireless sensor networks: A survey,' Journal of network and computer applications, vol. 52, pp. 101-115.

34. Giotis, K, Argyropoulos, C, Androulidakis, G, Kalogeras, D & Maglaris, V 2014, 'Combining OpenFlow and sFlow for an effective and scalable anomaly detection and mitigation mechanism on SDN environments,' Computer Networks, vol. 62, pp. 122-136.

35. Guo, Q, Li, X., Xu, G & Feng, Z 2017, 'MP-MID: Multi-Protocol Oriented Middleware-level Intrusion Detection method for wireless sensor networks,' Future Generation Computer Systems, vol. 70, pp. 42-47.

36. Gurung, S & Chauhan, S 2018,'A novel approach for mitigating gray hole attack in MANET,' Wireless Networks, vol. 24, no. 2, pp. 565-579.

37. Haider, W, Creech, G, X ie, Y & Hu, J 2016,'Windows based data sets for evaluation of robustness of host based intrusion detection systems (IDS) to zero-day and stealth attacks,'Future Internet, vol. 8, no. 3, pp. 1-8.

38. Hajisalem, V & Babaie, S 2018, 'A hybrid intrusion detection system based on ABC- AFS algorithm for misuse and anomaly detection,' Computer Networks, vol. 136, pp. 37-50.

39. Hamami, L & Nassereddine, B 2019, 'A Study of the Main Factors Wireless Sensor Networks,' In 2019 Third International conference on I-SMAC (IoT in Social, Mobile, A nalytics and Cloud), (I-SMAC), pp. 211-215.

40. Han, G, Shen, W, Duong, TQ, Guizani, M & Hara, T 2014,'A proposed security scheme against Denial of Service attacks in cluster-based wireless sensor networks,' Security and Communication Networks, vol. 7, no. 12, pp. 2542-2554.

41. Hoyos Ll, MS, Isaza E, GA, Vélez, JI & Castillo OL 2016, 'Distributed denial of service (ddos) attacks detection using machine learning prototype. In Distributed Computing and Artificial Intelligence,' 13th International Conference pp. 33-41.

42. Hu, S, Han, J, Wei, X & Chen, Z 2015, 'A multi-hop heterogeneous clusterbased optimization algorithm for wireless sensor networks,' Wireless Networks, vol. 21, no. 1, pp. 57-65.

43. J adaun, A, Alaria, SK & Saini, Y 2021,'Comparative study and design light weight data security system for secure data transmission in internet of things,'International J ournal on Recent and Innovation Trends in Computing and Communication, vol. 9, no. 3, pp. 28-32.

44. J an, MA, Nanda, P, He, X & L iu, RP 2018,'A Sybil attack detection scheme for a forest wildfire monitoring application,' Future Generation Computer Systems, vol. 80, pp. 613-626.

45. Jianjian, D, Yang, T & Feiyue, Y 2018, 'A novel intrusion detection system based on IABRBFSV M for wireless sensor networks,' Procedia computer science, vol. 131, pp. 1113-1121.

46. Kakatkar, C & Spann, M 2019, 'Marketing analytics using anonymized and fragmented tracking data,' International Journal of Research in Marketing, vol. 36, no. 1, pp. 117-136.

47. Kapusta, K, Memmi, G & Noura, H 2019, 'Additively homomorphic encryption and fragmentation scheme for data aggregation inside unattended wireless sensor networks,' Annals of Telecommunications, vol. 74, no. 3, pp.157-165.

48. Kato, K & Klyuev, V 2014, 'An intelligent ddos attack detection system using packet analysis and support vector machine,' IJICR, vol. 14, no. 5, pp.1-8.

49. Kato, K & Klyuev, V 2014, 'Large-scale network packet analysis for intelligent DDoS attack detection development,' In The 9th International Conference for Internet Technology and Secured Transactions (ICITST-2014), pp. 360-365.

50. Khalaf, OI & Sabbar, BM 2019, 'An overview on wireless sensor networks and optimal location of nodes,' Periodicals of Engineering and Natural Sciences (PEN), vol. 7, no. 3, pp. 1096-1101.

51. Kuang, F, Zhang, S, Jin, Z & Xu, W 2015, 'A novel SVM by combining kernel principal component analysis and improved chaotic particle swarm optimization for intrusion detection,' Soft Computing vol. 19, no. 5, pp. 1187-1199.

52. Kuo, YW, Li, CL, Jhang, JH & Lin, S 2018, 'Design of a wireless sensor network-based IoT platform for wide area and heterogeneous applications,' IEEE Sensors Journal, vol. 18, no. 12, pp.5187-5197.

53. Landaluce, H, Arjona, L, Perallos, A, Falcone, F, Angulo, I & Muralter, F 2020, 'A review of IoT sensing applications and challenges using RFID and wireless sensor networks,' Sensors, vol. 20, no. 9, pp. 1-8.

54. Lee, CC 2020, 'Security and privacy in wireless sensor networks,' Advances and challenges, Sensors, vol. 20, no. 3, pp 1-3.

55. Li, W, Yi, P, Wu, Y, Pan, L & Li, J 2014, 'A new intrusion detection system based on KNN classification algorithm in wireless sensor network,' Journal of Electrical and Computer Engineering, vol. 2014, no. 240217, pp. 1-8.

56. Lim, KW., Kapusta, K, Memmi, G & Jung, WS 2020, 'Multi-hop Data Fragmentation in Energy Harvesting Wireless Sensor Networks,' In 2020 Global Internet of Things Summit (GIoTS), IEEE, Dublin, Ireland. pp. 1-6.

57. Liu, S, Wang, L, Qin, J, Guo, Y & Zuo, H 2018, 'An intrusion detection model based on IPSO-SVM algorithm in wireless sensor network,' Journal of Internet Technology, vol. 19, no. 7, pp. 2125-2134.

58. Liu, X, Obaidat, MS, Lin, C, Wang, T & Liu, A 2020, 'Movement-based solutions to energy limitation in wirelessensor networks,' State of the art and future trends. IEEE Network, vol. 35, no. 2, pp. 188-193.

59. Liu, Z, Wei, W, Wang, H, Zhang, Y, Zhang, Q & Li, S 2018, 'Intrusion detection based on parallel intelligent optimization feature extraction and distributed fuzzy clustering in WSNs,' IEEE Access, vol. 6, pp. 72201-72211.

60. Lu, X, Han, D, Duan, L & Tian, Q 2020, 'Intrusion detection of wireless sensor networks based on IPSO algorithm and BP neural network,' International Journal of Computational Science and Engineering, vol. 22, no. 3, pp. 221-232.

61. Ma, T, Wang, F, Cheng, J, Yu, Y & Chen, X 2016, 'A hybrid spectral clustering and deep neural network ensemble algorithm for intrusion detection in sensor networks,' Sensors, vol. 16, no. 10, pp. 1-23.

62. MALEH, Y & Ezzati, A 2015, 'Lightweight Intrusion Detection Scheme for Wireless Sensor Networks,' IAENG International Journal of Computer Science, vol. 42, no. 4, pp. 347-354.

63. Manasa, D. 2022 'Energy Efficient Single Path with Multi Hop Routing Protocol for Mobile Coordinated Wireless Sensor Networks,' International Journal of Engineering and Technical Research, vol. 10, no. 2, pp. 1-6.

64. Mazur, K, Ksiezopolski, B & Nielek, R 2016, 'Multilevel modeling of distributed denial of service attacks in wireless sensor networks,' Journal of Sensors, vol. 2016, no. 5017248, pp. 1-13.

65. Medjadba, Y & Sahraoui, S 2016, 'Intrusion Detection System to Overcome a Novel Form of Replay Attack (Data Replay) in Wireless Sensor Networks,' International Journal of Computer Network & Information Security, vol. 8, no. 7, pp. 50-60.

66. Meena, G & Choudhary, RR 2017,'A review paper on IDS classification using K DD 99 and NSL K DD dataset in WEKA In 2017 International Conference on Computer, Communications and Electronics (Comptelix), pp. 553-558

67. Moreaux, G, Lemoine, FG, Argus, DF, Santamaría-Gómez, A, Willis, P, Soudarin, L & Ferrage, P 2016,'Horizontal and vertical velocities derived from the IDS contribution to ITRF2014, and comparisons with geophysical models,' Geophysical Journal International, vol. 207, no. 1, pp. 209-227.

68. Mrugala, K , Tuptuk, N & Hailes, S 2017,'Evolving attackers against wireless sensor networks using genetic programming, ' IET Wireless Sensor Systems, vol. 7, no. 4, pp.113-122.

69. Nápoles, G, Grau, I, Falcon, R, Bello, R &Vanhoof, K 2016,'A granular intrusion detection system usingrough cognitive networks,' In Recent advances in computational intelligence in defense and security, Springer International Publishing , Cham, pp. 169-191.

70. Nawaz, SA, Li, J , Bhatti, UA, Mehmood, A, A hmed, R & Ul Ain, Q 2020, 'A novel hybrid discrete cosine transform speeded up robust featurebased secure medical image watermarking algorithm,' Journal of Medical Imaging and Health Informatics, vol. 10, no. 11, pp. 2588-2599.

71. Osanaiye, O, Alfa, AS & Hancke, GP 2018, 'A statistical approach to detect jamming attacks in wireless sensor networks,' Sensors, vol. 18, no. 6, pp.1-15.

72. Pant, N, Singh, MP &Kumar, P 2014, 'Traffic &resource based methods for congestioncontrol in wireless sensor networks,' A comparative analysis. In 2014 IEEE 6th International Conference on Adaptive Science and Technology (ICAST), pp. 1-6.

73. Park, K, Song, Y & Cheong, YG 2018,'Classification of attack types for intrusion detection systems using a machine learning algorithm,' In 2018 IEEE Fourth International Conference on Big Data Computing Service and Applications (BigDataService), pp. 282-286.

74. Rahim, R 2017,'Man-in-the-middle-attack prevention using interlock protocol method,' ARPN J. Eng. Appl. Sci, vol. 12, no. 22, pp. 6483-6487.

75. Rajesh, M & Gnanasekar, JM 2016, 'Congestion control using aodv protocol scheme for wireless ad-hoc network,' Advances in Computer Science and Engineering, vol. 16, no. 1/2, pp.19-37.

76. Rao, NT, Bhattacharyya, D, Rao, VM & Kim, TH 2018,'Black Hole Attacks on WSNs Using Discrete Simulator: An Extensive Review,' International Journal of Grid and Distributed Computing, vol. 11, no. 12, pp. 33-42.

77. Rehman, AU, Rehman, SU & Raheem, H 2019,'Sinkhole Attacks in Wireless Sensor Networks: A Survey,' Wireless Personal Communications, vol. 106, no. 4, pp. 2291-2313.

78. Ren, J, Zhang, Y, Zhang, K & Shen, X 2016, 'Adaptive and channel-aware detection of selective forwarding attacks in wireless sensor networks,' IEEE Transactions on Wireless Communications, vol. 15, no. 5, pp. 3718-3731.

79. Riecker, M, Biedermann, S & Hollick, M 2013, 'Lightweight energy consumption based intrusion detection system for wireless sensor networks,' In Proceedings of the 28th Annual ACM Symposium on Applied Computing, pp.1784-1791.

80. Rost, P, Berberana, I, Maeder, A, Paul, H, Suryaprakash, V, Valenti, M, Wübben, D, Dekorsy, A & Fettweis, G 2015, 'Benefits &challenges of virtualization in 5G radio access networks,' IEEE Communications Magazine, vol. 53, no. 12, pp.75-82.

81. Sabri, Y & El Kamoun, N 2016, 'GRPW-MuS-s: a secure enhanced trust aware routing against wormhole attacks in wireless sensor networks,' Network, vol. 6, no. 5, pp. 56-59.

82. Safaldin, M, Otair, M & Abualigah, L 2021, 'Improved binary gray wolf optimizer and SV M for intrusion detection system in wireless sensor networks,' Journal of ambient intelligence and humanized computing, vol. 12, no. 2, pp. 1559-1576.

83. Saghar, K , Tari q, M, Kendall, D & Bouridane, A 2016, 'RAEED: A formally verified solution to resolve sinkhole attack in Wireless Sensor Network,' In 2016 13th International Bhurban Conference on A pplied Sciences and Technology (IBCAST), pp. 334-345.

84. Sahasrabuddhe, A, Naikade, S, Ramaswamy, A, Sadliwala, B & Futane, P 2017,' Survey on intrusion detection system using data mining techniques,Int Res J Eng Technol, vol. 4, no. 5, pp. 1780-4

85. Saleh, Y N, Chibelushi, CC, A bdel-Hamid, AA & Soliman, AH 2020,'Privacy Preservation for Wireless Sensor Networks in Healthcare,' State of the Art, and Open Research Challenges. arXiv preprint arX iv:2012.12958. pp. 1-42.

86. Sarigiannidis, P, Karapistoli, E & Economides, AA 2015, 'Detecting Sybil attacks in wireless sensor networks using U WB ranging-based information,' Expert Systems with A pplications, vol. 42, no. 21, pp. 7560-7572.

87. Sergiou, C, Vassiliou, V & Paphitis, A 2014,'Congestion control in wireless sensor networks through dynamic alternative path selection,'Computer Networks, vol. 75, pp. 226-238.

88. Shahryari, M & Naji, HR 2015, 'A cluster based approach for wormhole attack detection in wireless sensor networks,' J ournal of A dvanced Computer Science & Technology, vol. 4, no. 1, pp. 95-102.

89. Shamshirband, S, A mini, A, A nuar, NB, K iah, MLM, Teh, Y W & Furnell, S 2014, 'D-FICCA: A density-based fuzzy imperialist competitive clustering algorithm for intrusion detection in wireless sensor networks,' Measurement, vol. 55, pp. 212-226.

90. Shamshirband, S, Patel, A, A nuar, NB, K iah, MLM & A braham, A 2014, 'Cooperative game theoretic approach using fuzzy Q-learning for detecting and preventing intrusions in wireless sensor networks,' Engineering A pplications of Artificial Intelligence, vol. 32, pp. 228-241.

91. Shanthi, S & Rajan, EG 2016, 'Comprehensive analysis of security attacks and intrusion detection system in wireless sensor networks,' In 2016 2nd International Conference on Next Generation Computing Technologies (NGCT), pp. 426-431.

92. Singh, S & Saini, HS 2021, 'Learning-based security technique for selective forwarding attack in clustered WSN,' Wireless Personal Communications, vol. 118, no. 1, pp. 789-814.

93. Soni, S & Shrivastava, M 2018, 'Novel learning algorithms for efficient mobile sink data collection using reinforcement learning in wireless sensor network,' Wireless Communications and Mobile Computing, vol. 2018, no. 7560167, pp. 1-13.

94. Srbinovska, M, Gavrovski, C, Dimcev, V, Krkoleva, A & Borozan, V 2015,'Environmental parameters monitoring in precision agriculture using wireless sensor networks,' Journal of cleaner production, vol. 88, pp. 297-307.

95. Stylidou, A, Zervopoulos, A, Alvanou, AG, Koufoudakis, G, Tsoumanis, G & Oikonomou, K 2020, 'Evaluation of epidemic-based information dissemination in a wireless network testbed,' Technologies, vol. 8, no. 3, pp. 1-14.

96. Subba, B, Biswas, S & Karmakar, S 2016, A neural network based system for intrusion detection and attack classification In 2016 Twenty Second National Conference on Communication(NCC), pp. 1-6

97. Subba, B, Biswas, S & Karmakar, S 2016, 'False alarm reduction in signature-based IDS: game theory approach,' Security and Communication Networks, vol. 9, no. 18, pp. 4863-4881.

98. Sun, X, Yan, B, Zhang, X & Rong, C 2015, 'An integrated intrusion detection model of cluster- based wireless sensor network,' PloS one, vol. 10, no. 10, pp. e0139513.

99. Tanyingyong, V, Olsson, R, Hidell, M & Sjödin, P 2021, 'Scalable IoT sensing systems with dynamic sinks,' IEEE Internet of Things Journal, vol. 9, no. 10, pp.7211-7227.

100. Thamilarasu, G 2015, 'Genetic algorithm based intrusion detection system for wireless body area networks,' In 2015 IEEE Symposium on Computers and Communication (ISCC), pp. 160-165.

101. Tiwari, M, Tiwari, A & Sukheja, D 2015, 'Modified hop count analysis algorithm (MHCAA) for preventing wormhole attack in WSN,' Communications, vol. 3, no. 3, pp. 6-10.

102. Tomić, I & McCann, JA 2017, 'A survey of potential security issues in existing wireless sensor network protocols,' IEEE Internet of Things Journal, vol. 4, no. 6, pp.1910-1923.

103. Tran-Thanh, B, Pham-Quoc, C & Thinh, TN 2018,'OpenFlow Switches with Integrated Tiny NIDS to Mitigate Network Attacks,' International Journal of Computer Engineering and Information Technology, vol. 10, no. 6, pp. 85-91.

104. Wang, Y, Meng, W, Li, W, Li, J, Liu, WX & Xiang, Y 2018,'A fog-based privacy-preserving approach for distributed signature-based intrusion detection,' Journal of Parallel and Distributed Computing, vol. 122, pp. 26-35.

105. Wiese, M, Nötzel, J & Boche, H 2016,'A channel under simultaneous jamming and eavesdropping attack—Correlated random coding capacities under strong secrecy criteria,' IEEE Transactions on Information Theory, vol. 62, no. 7, pp. 3844-3862.

106. Yang, H & Chang, Y 2014, 'App-DDoS detection method based on K-means multiple principal component analysis,' Journal on Communication, vol. 35, no.5, pp. 16-24.

107. Yang, Y, Xu, HQ, Gao, L, Yuan, Y B, McLaughlin, K & Sezer, S 2016, Multidimensional intrusion detection system for IEC 61850-based SCADA networks,'IEEE Transactions on Power Delivery, vol. 32, no. 2, pp. 1068-1078.

108. Zarpelão, BB, Miani, RS, Kawakani, CT & de Alvarenga, SC 2017,'A survey of intrusion detection in Internet of Things,' Journal of Network and Computer Applications, vol. 84, pp. 25-37.

109. Zhang, W, Han, D, Li, KC & Massetto, FI 2020, 'Wireless sensor network intrusion detection system based on MK-ELM,' Soft Computing, vol. 24, no. 16, pp. 12361-12374.

LIST OF PUBLICATIONS

International Journal

1. Prabhu, T N & Karuppasamy, K 2022, 'Intrusion aware data transmission framework in wireless sensor network', Journal of Intelligent & Fuzzy Systems, vol. 43, no. 5, pp. 5721-5731, Impact Factor: 1.737.

www.ingramcontent.com/pod-product-compliance
Lightning Source LLC
LaVergne TN
LVHW082342200926
848481LV00012B/3423
* 9 7 9 8 2 3 1 4 7 5 7 3 5 *